CW00486978

CORAM SHAKESPEARE SCHOOLS FOUNDATION

Coram Shakespeare Schools Foundation (CSSF) is a cultural education charity working in schools across the UK. Its mission is to transform lives through the unique power of Shakespeare.

Best known for its flagship project, the Shakespeare Schools Festival, CSSF engages thousands of pupils every year from every community, background and school type, from inner-city secondaries to rural primaries, SEND settings and pupil referral units. The Festival aims to build confidence, life skills and cultural capital, and culminates in exhilarating performance evenings in professional theatres nationwide.

Every year, the games and exercises in this book are brought to life in schools across the UK, in workshops, rehearsals and teacher training. Collected together here, they will take the transformative power of CSSF's process to a larger audience.

CSSF is part of Coram, the UK's first and oldest children's charity, and now a group of specialist organisations working in the UK and around the world to change children's lives for the better.

ALANNA BEEKEN

Alanna Beeken is an English and Drama graduate, charity director and prolific reader. She was born in Kenya and has lived in five countries and counting. Alanna spent eight years working at Coram Shakespeare Schools Foundation. She continues to work in arts education and is passionate about creativity and the power of play in learning.

DRAMA GAMES is a series of books for teachers, workshop leaders and directors in need of new and dynamic activities when working with actors in education, workshop or rehearsal.

Also available in this series:

DRAMA GAMES FOR ACTORS
Thomasina Unsworth

DRAMA GAMES FOR CLASSROOMS AND WORKSHOPS
Jessica Swale

DRAMA GAMES FOR CLOWNING AND PHYSICAL COMEDY
Joe Dieffenbacher

DRAMA GAMES FOR DEVISING
Jessica Swale

DRAMA GAMES FOR REHEARSALS
Jessica Swale

DRAMA GAMES FOR THOSE WHO LIKE TO SAY NO
Chris Johnston

DRAMA GAMES FOR YOUNG CHILDREN
Katherine Zachest

And more to follow…

The publisher welcomes suggestions for further titles in the series.

Alanna Beeken

coram
SHAKESPEARE
SCHOOLS FOUNDATION

drama games

FOR EXPLORING SHAKESPEARE

Foreword by Paterson Joseph

Edited by Francesca Ellis

NICK HERN BOOKS
London
www.nickhernbooks.co.uk

A Nick Hern Book

DRAMA GAMES
FOR EXPLORING SHAKESPEARE

First published in Great Britain in 2023
by Nick Hern Books Limited
The Glasshouse, 49a Goldhawk Road,
London W12 8QP

Designed and typeset by Nick Hern Books, London
Printed and bound in Great Britain by
Severn, Gloucester

A CIP catalogue record for this book
is available from the British Library

ISBN 978 1 84842 942 0

MIX
Paper from
responsible sources
FSC® C022174

CARBON NEUTRAL

FOREWORD

The first time I ever directed a play was for a television documentary called *My Shakespeare*. I had been asked to tackle one of Shakespeare's plays in a place I knew well from my past. I chose *Romeo and Juliet*, and I controversially chose Harlesden in North West London, an area most known at the time for poverty, crime and social deprivation. As with almost all media assessments of places that are supposedly 'notorious', that picture, I knew, was altogether wrong, based largely on easy clichés and old tropes of urban degeneration.

And, true enough, what I found in those four short weeks of rehearsals and performance was quite the opposite of the myth. My band of eighteen brothers and sisters, all first-time actors and, most challengingly, first-time Shakespeareans, came through the period of introduction, rehearsal and eventual performance of Shakespeare at RADA with flying colours; as easily witnessed by everyone who watched the Channel 4 broadcast in 2005. This group of eighteen- to fifty-two-year-olds blew many people away with their commitment and understanding of Shakespeare's star-crossed lovers and the world they inhabited; transposed to their own area and made real for them because it spoke to the issues of division and love that mirrored their lives. It was an experience that transformed a number of lives, including my own.

One of the missing ingredients at that time, however, was a blueprint for attempting what was an almost impossible task, freighted with many traps and snares. To teach people who were mildly terrified, a little hostile and deeply underconfident about their ability to understand, learn and perform the works of the world's most important and influential playwright, that Shakespeare was for them, too. What I would have dearly loved was a book like Coram Shakespeare Schools Foundation's *Drama Games for Exploring Shakespeare.*

This wonderful book will be an invaluable resource for anyone approaching the teaching or directing of Shakespeare, whether novice or veteran. Whenever I've tried to introduce Shakespeare to a new group of people, I get out a file of loose leaves of paper with various exercises, notes and modifications. At last, here is a ready-made resource in one helpful package. CSSF manages to make the introduction of Shakespearean language and attitudes, stagecraft and themes seem effortless and simple for anyone. With the easy-to-read, at-a-glance format, CSSF has provided a survival manual for any teacher or director attempting to coax a shy group into letting rip on some four-hundred-year-old text. Quite the feat.

I can readily imagine using these easy-to-follow exercises in a setting that requires a lot of flexibility due to the players' age and ability. It can be tricky getting children engaged in Shakespeare, for example, if they feel the language is beyond them; this book neatly swerves this potential obstacle by making the use of everyday phrases sound as if Shakespeare were our contemporary.

The sections where we are given the aim of each game is brilliant. So often what is already a daunting and seemingly mysterious world is made more, not less, scary by exercises that seem complex and equally obscure. That is not the case with this book. CSSF's approach will allow anyone to tackle Shakespeare's myriad themes and phrases, poetry and prose as easily as reeling off a list of things you had for breakfast. Iambic pentameter, caesuras, thought changes during long speeches and even the complex physicality of stagecraft, are so woven into these games that players will have mastered much of these previously alien concepts before they are even aware. And they'll be laughing and most importantly *playing* while they do this. 'The *play*'s the thing...': an invaluable lesson that my rather glamorous mentor on *My Shakespeare*, Baz Luhrmann, reminded me during a tricky section of that rehearsal process.

Some exercises will make for hilarity, some will move us with their simple truth, but all of them will help ignite the imagination of the players, no matter what their ability and experience. I wish I had this to hand when I was first teaching students about the accessibility of William Shakespeare's stories and words. But, better late than never, in my case.

Paterson Joseph
London, 2023

Paterson Joseph is a Patron of Coram Shakespeare Schools Foundation and is well known for his Shakespearean roles, including Troilus in *Troilus and Cressida*, Oswald in *King Lear*, Dumaine in *Love's Labour's Lost* and Brutus in *Julius Caesar*, all for the Royal Shakespeare Company.

Paterson's theatre credits include Scrooge in *A Christmas Carol* (The Old Vic), Tshembe Matoseh in *Les Blancs* (Best Actor, Barclays TMA Awards, Royal Exchange, Manchester) and Brutus Jones in *The Emperor Jones* (National Theatre). His TV and film credits include *Peep Show* (Objective), *Green Wing* (BAFTA Winner Pioneer Award, Talkback), *Noughts + Crosses* and *Vigil* (BBC), *The Beach* (Figment Films) and *Wonka* (Warner Bros).

Paterson is the Chancellor of Oxford Brookes University and his debut novel, *The Secret Diaries of Charles Ignatius Sancho* (Dialogue), was published in 2022.

CONTENTS

INTRODUCTION

Shakespeare sticks. His words are more than four hundred years old, but his stories continue to be told on stages and in classrooms, on screens and in books across the world. No matter the time and distance between us and when he was writing, Shakespeare's work says something about the human condition that keeps us coming back for more. He wrote characters grappling with life's biggest questions and the myriad complications of relationships, emotion and power. He created language so beautiful, funny and interesting that it has been assimilated into our everyday speech – when is the last time you were in a pickle? Or on a wild goose chase? What about swaggering, puking or ranting? Since he first put quill to page, in every era, all over the world, Shakespeare sticks.

> 'They started to love the Shakespearean language – lines like, "turn hell-hound turn" and "Out damn spot." I think they liked that the language is a bit naughty. They enjoyed the way Shakespeare played with the language.'
> *Laura Hodgkiss, teacher, St Anne's Catholic Primary School, Knowsley*

Coram Shakespeare Schools Foundation

Coram Shakespeare Schools Foundation (CSSF) uses these iconic stories and brilliant words to inspire new generations. We are a cultural education charity that uses Shakespeare to empower children of all abilities through workshops, classroom resources and the unique opportunity to perform on a professional stage. CSSF runs the world's largest youth drama festival, the annual Shakespeare Schools Festival. Founded in 2000 with just eight schools, we have grown to work with hundreds of schools across the UK each year, training teachers to direct abridged Shakespeare plays for performance in a professional theatre.

Shakespeare is an inspiration and an icon, but he is not the whole point of what we do. We use Shakespeare's work as a vehicle for fostering the skills needed to survive in an ever-changing world – communication, resilience, confidence and teamwork. In my eight years of working with the charity I have borne witness to hundreds of young lives transformed by the challenge of performing Shakespeare.

> 'Our school is situated in a hard community. There is gun crime, knife crime and problems with drugs. Children's home lives can be chaotic and many of them see quite negative things. By taking part in the festival, children realise they can achieve. They aspire to greater things and have the ambition to pursue their dreams. The confidence and communication skills they gain equip them for life in the big wide world.'
> *Joanna Mously, head teacher, Saints Peter and Paul Roman Catholic Primary School, Kirkby*

Our Principles

Decades of working with students and teachers of every background and ability has shaped CSSF's approach to theatremaking and learning, and given us a fantastic catalogue of games. We know how to use Shakespeare to inspire and challenge everyone. These are our guiding principles, which underpin the design of the games and exercises in this book:

1. Shakespeare is for everyone

> 'All the world's a stage, and all the men and women merely players.' *As You Like It*

At the heart of our philosophy is our belief that Shakespeare is for everyone, no matter their age or culture, background or ability. In his time, Shakespeare wrote for all of society – his casts of characters range from commoner to king, and his words worked as well (if not better) for the groundlings at the actors' feet as for the lords and ladies in the seats. CSSF has reimagined this spirit of inclusion for the modern age, working with a diverse array of people including those with profound physical and educational needs.

> 'For children with life-limiting conditions at our school, every second counts. We want to give them every drop of joy that life can bring. The fact that they are up on a professional stage performing Shakespeare is incredible. You see their faces light up. It's something that most parents would never have dreamed possible.'
> *Gail Pascoe, teacher, Knockevin Special School, County Down*

Often the most inspired and creative choices in performance are born from the challenges faced in the rehearsal room – what could be perceived as a disability inspires a brilliant piece of stagecraft, or a very large cast creates a fantastic ensemble world together. I have lost count of the nights I have sat in the CSSF audience, captivated by a piece of theatre that was fantastic because of (and not in spite of) the challenges faced by its actors. If you have any doubts about your actors' ability to tackle Shakespeare, or indeed your own, use this book to banish them. Shakespeare gives us the opportunity to surprise ourselves and everyone else with what we can do.

2. The power of play and kinaesthetic learning

> 'Joy's soul lies in the doing' *Troilus and Cressida*

Shakespeare's stories resonate with young people (and everyone) because they are playful, magical, funny and silly, as well as moving and thought-provoking. So many are turned off Shakespeare because they first encounter his work on the page, silently read and never spoken. Shakespeare wrote for actors and audiences, not scholars and academics, and his words were meant to be spoken aloud and played with. His spirit of mischief and play dances through even his most serious tragedies – and play is the most important part of our process too. Every game in this book puts fun first, and Shakespeare naturally follows.

> 'I never knew that I could do Shakespeare! It was so fun, I enjoyed the warm-ups and dancing to music. But my favourite part was performing on stage. Now I am more confident to try something new.'
> *Alesha, 9, student, Old Catton Junior School, Norwich*

Years of working with actors of all ages has showed us that most people learn best through doing. Moving, speaking and playing with Shakespeare brings it to life in a way that sitting at a desk, struggling to read the unfamiliar and complex language never could. Every game in this book is designed to be played actively, making use of space and bodies and learning from the outside in.

3. Shared ownership

> 'Now let's go hand in hand, not one before another.' *The Comedy of Errors*

Our years of trial and error in classrooms and on stages have led us to our own definition of a director – we see a director as a facilitator. This is how we hope you will approach these games too. A facilitator will inspire and harness the creativity of their actors, rather than create a show to serve their own vision. These games are designed in this spirit – to create a sense of group ownership and ignite the imaginations of the participants.

> 'Some people say Shakespeare is challenging. I say, life in general is challenging. If you don't give young people a challenge, how are they ever going to learn? Even if you find it difficult, even if you make a mistake, you're always learning. All the big themes – death and love and conflict – are there. There's no point hiding them from young people. We're going to discover them anyway for ourselves, so you might as well give us the chance to think them through in a safe space.'
> *Ibrahim, 16, student, Morpeth School, Bethnal Green*

We want young people to feel that Shakespeare belongs to them, and to find a connection to the words that resonates for them in their own time. This means that we are often irreverent in our approach, cutting up scripts (sometimes literally), experimenting with language and playing with characters and ideas. Many of our games focus on this, mining the script for connections to the players and seeking opportunities to inspire them.

Who is This Book For?

The games in this book make Shakespeare fun and accessible for anyone, no matter their knowledge of Shakespeare. At Coram Shakespeare Schools Foundation, we work with teachers and students aged 8 to 18, but these games can be used and adapted for most ages and abilities. You might be a director or a teacher, a student or an actor. You might be tackling Shakespeare for the very first time or be well-versed in his works. You could use this book to support your direction of a Shakespeare play, bringing playfulness to your rehearsal room, or you might be an English teacher wanting to bring the text to life in the classroom.

CSSF trains directors and we have structured the book as though you are working towards a performance. If you are directing a Shakespeare play, with a cast of any age and experience, we hope it will give you a structure and momentum for your rehearsals.

However, you could just as easily pick it up and flick through it for one-off games to enliven a lesson, support a monologue or introduce Shakespeare to your drama club. We have tried to make our games as inclusive as possible, and in some cases have suggested variations or extensions to suit different ages and abilities. However, every company is unique, and you know your actors best, so feel free to find your own adaptations.

HOW TO USE THIS BOOK

The games are grouped into the following chapters:

- **Warm-ups and General Games** are the perfect place to start a session or rehearsal process. They will create all the conditions you need to establish a way of working and playing together.
- **Story and World-building** includes games to explore the events, environments and societies of Shakespeare's plays.
- **Introducing Shakespeare's Language** will help you break down the text, supporting players to find their own connection to the words.
- **Activating Shakespeare's Language** goes further, to liberate actors from the script and connect the words on the page to their movement and voice.
- **Character** illuminates actors' choices to develop interesting, believable performances.
- **Staging** focuses on big ensemble moments that might be challenging to stage, offering simple games that empower every performer.

Within each section, the games build on each other, and each section follows naturally from the last. However, we advocate a cyclical rehearsal process with experimentation and play at its core, so don't feel bound by the structure that we have chosen. You can dip in and out of sections as you need, and we recommend returning regularly to the general games.

You do not need to be a Shakespeare expert to facilitate the games here, but some of them will require a bit of preparation. Even if you don't have time to read a whole play, knowing the story you are focusing on, understanding your characters, remembering some key lines and preparing some resources will help you make the most of the games. We will let you know when and how much preparation is necessary. Each game in this book also comes with a panel including the minimum number of players, the youngest age that we feel can play the game, the length of time it might take to play, and the key skills it explores. All of this information is offered as a guide only; you know your group and what is appropriate for them.

We encourage you to approach every game in a spirit of play and collaboration. Our work is non-competitive, and we have carried that principle through in the design of our rehearsal games. Where the games have an element of competition, we encourage you to harness this spirit for positive ends and not focus on winning and losing. It may be helpful to facilitate a discussion about the meaning of collaboration and ensemble work.

NOTES AND GLOSSARY

Authorship – We do not claim singular ownership over the games in these pages. CSSF is a melting pot of ideas, we find inspiration in theatremakers, teachers, partners, and most of all in the young people we work with. This is a recipe book of our most effective Shakespeare-inspired games, based on years of experience and with thanks to countless advisers and collaborators. Some games are well-known, but have been given a Shakespearean twist.

Safety – Where a game can get lively or physically risky, please pass these cautions on to your players. Acting can make you feel vulnerable, particularly when we ask players to connect emotionally with characters and stories. We encourage you to build focus slowly and to encourage incremental growth in trust and engagement from your players.

Active audiences – Some games are designed to be played by a few specific actors rather than everyone, but the whole cast can be involved as an active audience. This means an audience that is watching critically, looking for things they like and ways to improve the performance. We encourage you to introduce this concept early on and use your cast as assistant directors. This will deepen their connection to the text and take some pressure off you as a solo facilitator.

Turning the dial up – This means the players making their voice or actions bigger, usually on a scale of 1 to 10.

World of the play – This refers to the particular setting and circumstances of the play that you are working with in any specific game. This often combines place (Verona, the English court, a forest at night) with cultural or social context (feuding families, loyalty to the king, the potential for magic). Some details are provided by Shakespeare, while others are devised, changed or updated by you and your company.

Ensemble – From the French, this word translates to 'together'. We use it to mean your whole cast or a large number of players working well together as one team.

ACKNOWLEDGEMENTS

CSSF's practice is a melting pot of contemporary rehearsal-room approaches, and we have been lucky enough to work, consult or brush shoulders with a host of magnificent directors and facilitators over the years.

The names below are those who have most closely created, tested and honed our content over the last decade. They are the tip of the iceberg; beyond them, thanks are due to everyone who has inspired us over the years, whose names would fill many more pages of this book.

Tim Allsop
Justin Audibert
Pete Collins
Louise de Froment
Natalie Diddams
Francesca Ellis
Rachel Ellis
Dominic Fitch
Jordana Golbourn
Guy Hargreaves
Lucy Hind
Kate Hughes
Lucy Kerbel
Iain Jones
Amy Leach
John Lightbody
Lucianne McEvoy Collins
Rebecca Manley
Claire Meade
Nicola Miles-Wildin
Brian Mullin
Maddie Short
Joanne Skapinker
Rich Weinman

PART ONE

WARM-UPS AND GENERAL GAMES

'The play's the thing'
Hamlet

These games are great for warming up your cast and preparing them for rehearsals, but they do much more than that. They will establish an atmosphere of focus, connection, support and fun – all the conditions needed for making great theatre. They will also help you to build an engaged and supportive ensemble, who are willing to take risks, be silly and help each other. We have put Shakespeare's characters and language at the heart of these games so that the intrinsic connection between Shakespeare and fun is clear.

These games can, and should, be used at any time in your process, not just at the start of rehearsals. You will find that they spark ideas, refresh a rehearsal room and lead to some of your best creative discoveries. Never underestimate the power of play – it is how we learn from the moment we are born.

I Am…

An inclusive game for building stage pictures and sparking creativity.

How to Play

Ask the group to get into a circle. Explain that you will be building some very quick pictures and that you are looking for imagination and instinct – encourage students not to second guess their own ideas.

To start, pick a scene/scenario from your play that's easily accessible to your whole cast, e.g. the wrestling match from *As You Like It*. You don't need to reference the play yet.

Ask actors to enter the circle one at a time to create a freeze-frame of this scene. They do this by saying 'I am a…' and then striking a pose, e.g. 'I am a champion wrestler' with fists in the air. The next person to step on to the stage should use this offer to build up the picture, e.g. 'I am the opponent.'

Encourage participants to be imaginative. They don't have to be a person, they can be anything that fits the scene, e.g. 'I am the bell that rings between rounds.'

Everyone should enter quickly and without fuss. After the image is complete, ask the actors what they enjoyed and what looked effective. You might like to ask one of them to suggest the next scene.

Once everyone has got the hang of this, introduce a more specific scene from your play, e.g. a masked ball in Verona, Richard III's castle, a magical forest clearing. You may like to introduce a line or two of Shakespeare to these freeze-frames.

The Aim of the Game

This game will get your cast used to working together to quickly create stage pictures. It will start them thinking about the world of your play and the characters and objects that might be present.

Players	Age	Time
5+	6+	15

Imagination, Improvisation, Storytelling, Teamwork

The King's Coming

A quick Shakespearean warm-up in a call-and-response style.

How to Play

Define where your playing space is and agree where the 'audience' are. Ask your cast to spread across the space and introduce the following instructions. When you call them out, the players follow them instantly.

- Take a bow.
- Upstage/downstage/stage-left/stage-right (actors move to that part of the stage).
- Wings (actors move to the side of the playing space and wait, ready to come on).
- The King's coming (actors go on one knee and say 'Your Majesty').
- A horse, a horse! (actors gallop round the space on an invisible horse).
- The rest is silence (actors perform the most dramatic death they can).

These are a starting point, you can create your own commands with your group based on a specific play, e.g. 'A drum! A drum!' or 'Fairies, skip hence!' These commands could form a useful shorthand for directing large ensemble scenes.

You can add an element of competition by saying the last person to perform the command, or the person who is least convincing in their performance, is out.

The Aim of the Game

This game will bring participants into the playful, larger-than-life mood of your rehearsal room. It warms up the body, increases focus at the start of a session, and helps young actors get accustomed to the terminology of stage space.

Players	Age	Time
2+	6+	10
Energy, Focus		

The Clapping Game

A playful, low-pressure way to create comedy on stage.

How to Play

Set up some random objects in the space, e.g. a coat, a chair, a hat, an umbrella.

Ask for a volunteer and explain that they will leave the room while the 'audience' decide on a simple task for them to do. As they get close to achieving the task the audience will let them know with applause. The closer they get, the more generous the applause will become.

Once they're out of the room, decide as a group what you want them to do. It will be tempting to invent something extravagant, so try to keep it simple, e.g. 'Put on this hat and stand on the chair.' Remind the 'audience' that they need to be clear and generous in their applause.

The actor re-enters and tries actions out until they arrive at the right action. You may need to raise the stakes by giving them a time limit. If time runs out it doesn't matter – the aim of the exercise is to find the comedy in their performance, which will happen with or without them finding the 'right' answer.

Ask students to reflect on what they enjoyed about watching this, and especially what made them laugh, e.g. the actor's openness, vulnerability, inventiveness, optimism or desperation. How can they harness these qualities in their own performances?

The Aim of the Game

Even the darkest of Shakespeare's tragedies contain moments of humour, and this game will ease young actors into performing things the audience find comical. They are not aiming to 'be funny' or required to have brilliant ideas, just to achieve their task, with the comedy rooted in the uncertainty of the character. It will encourage participants to think like directors and seek out moments that would work on stage.

Variations and Extensions

For two players

Shakespeare loved to exploit the humour of the audience being in on a secret. This game is useful when you have a comedic scene played by two characters with differing intentions, e.g. the yellow-stocking scene between Malvolio and Olivia in *Twelfth Night*.

In this case, the volunteers who leave the room could be the actors playing the characters. Before they leave the room, give them a secret note, e.g.:

- (Malvolio) You are deeply attracted to the other person on stage.
- (Olivia) You are repelled by the other person on stage.

These notes would work for moments in many of Shakespeare's plays, e.g. *A Midsummer Night's Dream*, *Much Ado About Nothing* or *Richard III*.

You might also give your actors an appropriate line each, which they can use at any time, e.g. 'Sweet Lady!' and 'This is very midsummer madness' for Malvolio and Olivia respectively.

Once the actors have left the room, reveal the notes to the audience so they are in on the joke.

Play *The Clapping Game* as before, with your characters trying to achieve a joint task decided by the audience, all the while playing their secret notes.

For multiple players

This is a version of the game where multiple volunteers leave the room, and works well when rehearsing group scenes, such as the Mechanicals in *A Midsummer Night's Dream*.

As with the two-player game, give each volunteer a secret note to play when they return. Some example notes are:

- Organise everyone.
- Shine – be the very best.
- Try not to be noticed.

- Smile at all times.
- Copy someone else.
- You're completely lost.

You could also invite each actor to choose a prop that they think suits their character. Simply giving an actor a prop – relevant or otherwise – can elicit lots of comedy from a scene.

When your volunteers leave the room, remind your audience that the joint task with so many players needs to be kept very simple, e.g. make a line at the back of the stage and take a bow.

These variations of *The Clapping Game* are great precursors to rehearsing specific scenes – you could run the scene 'straight' immediately after the game, keeping the qualities you have just discovered, or if your actors know their lines you could try inserting dialogue into the game.

Players	Age	Time
5+	10+	20
Characterisation, Improvisation, Teamwork		

Who's the Leader?

A game that will help participants focus and work together.

How to Play

Ask players to come into in a circle and start a flowing sequence of slow movements, e.g. tapping your head, waving gently. Ask everybody to copy you. Once you are all in the flow of the movement it should look like no one is leading. Once participants are comfortable with this exercise, ask for a volunteer to leave the room, so that they can come back and guess the leader.

Once the person is outside, ask somebody to become the new leader. Now everyone should copy their movements. Encourage the group to look at each other and not necessarily the secret leader. The volunteer should come back once the movement sequence has started and position themselves in the middle of the circle. They can have three guesses to identify who the leader is.

Once the group is confident with the game, ask leaders to make the movement specific to a moment or location in your play, such as preparing for battle, enjoying a feast or getting ready for a party.

The Aim of the Game

This is a great exercise to focus your cast, build trust and get them working together as a team. It also provides opportunities for students to lead a group non-verbally. It could be used to stage a big ensemble movement piece – see also *Flock of Birds* (game 62).

Players	Age	Time
7+	6+	10
Focus, Physicality, Rhythm, Teamwork		

Shakespeare Sign Names

A gentle introduction to each other and Shakespeare's characters.

How to Play

Ask everyone to come into a circle and create their own sign name. Your sign name is an action which you perform to represent you – it can be something that you like, a hobby that you have, or something about your appearance. Sign names should use hands and facial expressions, e.g. miming mixing a cake, smoothing your hair, or stroking a pet.

Everyone signs their name in turn round the circle, also explaining why they have chosen this sign. The group copies each sign name, so that the person signing sees their name reflected back by the group.

Now the games can begin. Ask participants to move around the room and introduce themselves to as many people as possible with their sign name.

Then, form a circle. You sign your own name, and then choose someone else in the circle and sign their name. That person signs their own name, and then someone else's, to pass it on. It is a game of memory and quick reactions – you can raise the stakes by saying players will be out if they can't remember another name or react quickly enough.

This game helps build familiarity with Shakespeare's characters. Students pick a character from their play and create a sign name for them – within the group you can have several of the same character, or ask them to pick character names out of a hat if you want to ensure variety. Now play as above.

The Aim of the Game

This is a good way to introduce characters to the cast and encourage them to begin thinking about their defining characteristics.

Players	Age	Time
6+	8+	15–20
Characterisation, Focus, Imagination, Memory		

Zounds!

A Shakespearean warm-up to get your cast focused.

How to Play

This is a variation on the well-known *Zip, Zap, Boing*. Start by teaching your cast the words and actions. We have made suggestions below but you can choose any short, fun Shakespearean words that you like and work with your students to invent actions. Ask everyone to come into a circle and tell them that you will be passing energy around from person to person. Layer in three commands:

- 'Zounds' – pass the energy in a clockwise direction around the circle. Add an action, such as turning and clapping in the direction of the energy.
- 'Forsooth' – pass the energy across the circle, being very clear who the recipient is. The action could be clasping your hands and pointing across.
- 'Have at thee' – reject the energy, so it goes back to the person who is sending it to you. The action could be holding both hands up in a 'stop' gesture.

Encourage players to be as precise as possible. You could add some competition by saying if they are too slow they will be out.

You could use language from your play, e.g.:

Romeo and Juliet – 'Montague', 'Capulet', 'I bite my thumb at thee'.

Macbeth – 'Double double', 'Lay on Macduff', Turn hell-hound'.

As you progress through rehearsals, encourage participants to lead this game themselves, choosing words and actions from the play that they enjoy.

The Aim of the Game

A fun, energetic warm-up game to inspire a playful use of Shakespeare's words.

Players	Age	Time
10+	8+	10
Energy, Focus, Rhythm, Voice		

Clap, Stamp, Shimmy

An energetic warm-up game to focus your cast.

How to Play

Ask players to get into pairs and set them the task of counting to three, alternating the numbers between them. It should follow the pattern below:

A: One.

B: Two.

A: Three.

B: One.

A: Two

B: Three… etc.

Reflect on their experience of the exercise. Perhaps it was harder than they expected? How did that feel? Reflect on why we don't like making mistakes and might judge ourselves when we do. You could take this opportunity to start a conversation about their attitudes to working with Shakespeare.

Set up the ethos of celebrating mistakes, explaining that the players should repeat the exercise but this time, when they make a mistake, they must celebrate wildly – clapping, whooping, bowing or dancing. They should still try their best, but understand that mistakes are an expected part of pushing ourselves beyond our comfort zone.

Repeat the exercise, but this time replace the number 'one' with a clap. Let them try this a few times, before also replacing 'two' with a stamp, then 'three' with a shimmy. Remind players to continue celebrating their failures.

Finally, ask participants to return to the numbers one, two, three. Before they begin, ask them to make a commitment in their pairs that this time they are going to be the best they can possibly be. It's still okay to make mistakes and celebrate them, but they should aim to be as brilliant as possible!

Ask who thought they were better at the exercise the final time? Reflect with them about how a task is easier when you get time to practise, are focused, working together, and aren't afraid to make mistakes and be ambitious for each other. It may seem counter-intuitive to them, but playing with their 'script' (adding the clap, stamp and shimmy) improved their 'performance' and made them more confident. This is an attitude we encourage you to take forward into all rehearsals.

The Aim of the Game

We believe that there are few ways to do Shakespeare 'wrong', and that actors should be encouraged to experiment with his work to discover their own connection to it. This game liberates players from the fear of failure that can come with tackling Shakespeare for the first time. It also demonstrates to participants the importance of teamwork and play in creating theatre.

Players	Age	Time
2+	8+	20

Energy, Focus, Rhythm, Teamwork

Venga Venga

A silly call-and-response to quickly introduce Shakespeare into your rehearsal room.

How to Play

Ask the group to get into a circle and teach them the following calls-and-responses:

- When I clap my hands once,
  You slap your thighs twice.
- When I say 'High!' (*reach up with a high voice*),
  You say 'Low!' (*reach down with a low voice*).
- When I say 'Venga Venga' (*raise two hands like crab claws and move them from left to right*),
  You say 'Hula Hula' (*spin an imaginary hula hoop round your waist*).
- When I say 'I'm looking for the man who shot my pa' (*cowboy-walk into the centre*),
  You say 'But darling I love you' (*1930s black-and-white movie voice, hand to heart*).
- Each call-and-response can work the other way, e.g. When I slap my thighs twice,
  You clap your hands once.

Remember to build up slowly so the cast gets the hang of one call-and-response before you teach them a new one. Don't be afraid to go for it, be bold and loud! Give yourself permission to play so that your cast can do the same.

Once you and your cast have played with this for a while, ask them to suggest lines or characters from your play that could work with this game. Ask for a phrase, tone of voice and accompanying gesture, and then a different phrase, tone and gesture in response. Try not to judge or alter your actors' suggestions too much so that they can quickly begin to feel ownership of their play and characters.

This can also be a useful way to help your company learn cues. If you have a whole-ensemble reaction moment (e.g. 'She knows the heat of a luxurious bed!'), make the call the cue line and the response the reaction (e.g. everyone gasping in shock). To prepare your company for speedy transitions, use the last line of the first scene as the call, and the first line of the next scene as the response.

The Aim of the Game

This game is quick and fun, and should set a playful tone for your rehearsals. It's a good way to get your actors thinking and reacting quickly, so keep it energised and make the cues speedy. It introduces Shakespeare's language and characters in a light-hearted, low-pressure way.

Players	Age	Time
5+	8+	10
Energy, Focus, Rhythm, Voice		

Ban Ban Caliban

A rhythmic warm-up for imaginations and bodies.

How to Play

Make a circle with your group and create a rhythm together by stamping feet, clapping hands or tapping knees, e.g. two slaps on your thighs followed by two hand claps. When the group is comfortable with the rhythm, teach the chant:

'Ban ban Caliban,
Has a new master,
Get a new man.
Now it's time for you to say,
How the monster looks today.'

Ask the group to give you some ideas of what a monster might look like. Encourage them to really stretch their imaginations beyond a 'traditional monster' – maybe it has soft fur, six pointy ears and long purple toenails.

Start the chant, and every time you say:

'Now it's time for you to say,
How the monster looks today.'

point to a pair or group of players to decide what part of the monster they will be. They then come into the circle, take an active shape of the monster's body part and tell the group what they are, e.g. 'We are the monster's sharp, pointy teeth.' Their shape should be alive and moving, e.g. snapping teeth. If they want, they can add a sound effect.

The group continues to build the monster using this chant. Ask players to think about how they can build on the monster in the middle and to consider where they will be in relation to other monster body parts. Once the monster is complete, the leader can ask the monster to breathe in and out, roar, sneeze, move a few steps – anything to bring this huge creature to life! You could also draw some big pictures of monster body parts for participants to hold as they make the shape, to help the group to visualise what they are creating.

Any couplet of lines can be used to create a chant and start to build characters, images or moments from the play. Rhyming couplets work particularly well. Some examples from other plays are:

- *Macbeth*
  'Double double toil and trouble,
  Fire burn and cauldron bubble,
  Now it's time for you to tell,
  What you're putting in the spell.'
- *A Midsummer Night's Dream*
  'Over hill, over dale,
  Through bush, through briar,
  We do wander everywhere!
  Now it's time for you to say,
  What character are you today?'

The Aim of the Game

A playful, physical way to fire up imaginations and encourage a playful approach to Shakespeare's language and characters.

Players	Age	Time
5+	6+	15
Energy, Focus, Imagination, Improvisation, Teamwork		

Character Swaps

A game to bond your cast and create a deeper understanding of character.

How to Play

Set up a circle of chairs, enough for every participant except yourself. If you are playing with one or more wheelchair users use spots on the floor instead.

You are in the middle of the circle, but you want a chair. You get one by making a true statement about yourself (beginning with the words 'Anyone who…') which may also be true for other people in the circle, e.g. 'Anyone who is wearing jeans.'

If you are sitting and the statement is true for you, you must find another place in the circle, e.g. everyone who is wearing jeans must find a new place. There will always be one person left in the middle to think of a new statement.

Before you begin, emphasise these three rules:

- You cannot push anyone from their seat.
- You cannot return to your seat once you've vacated it.
- You cannot swap to the seat immediately next to yours.

Once the game has been going a minute or two, pause it and ask that, from now on, statements relate to Shakespeare. Participants can talk about his plays, him as a person, their studying of Shakespeare, characters in his plays, etc. Anything, as long as it is still a true statement that can be shared (e.g. 'Anyone who sometimes finds Shakespeare's language difficult to understand.' 'Anyone who has ever seen a Shakespeare play.' 'Anyone who thinks Juliet is too good for Romeo.') This will help your cast find common ground with each other and give you a bit of information about their knowledge on and attitude towards Shakespeare.

Finally, ask players to make statements in character. Now actors must swap chairs when statements are true for their character, not themselves (e.g. 'Anyone who falls in love/is a Capulet/dies.') You could also ask the group to think about how their character would move across the circle. As they swap, ask them to react to the others, e.g. if Macbeth and the witches cross paths, how will they look at each other? How might they interact? Which emotions will they show? Alternatively, you could allocate groups of participants homogenous characters, e.g. the fairies, the lovers, the Mechanicals, Montagues or Capulets, to begin to differentiate between individuals. This is a useful way to familiarise the group with the characters and begin to think about what happens when different characters are on stage together.

The Aim of the Game

Creating a brilliant performance of Shakespeare begins with creating a strong, bonded ensemble who know each other and their characters well. This game ticks all those boxes, and is a fun way to start rehearsals and get the cast into a playful mindset.

Players	Age	Time
10+	8+	15
Characterisation, Energy, Focus, Teamwork		

Who's the Boss?

An energetic game to get your cast thinking about clear storytelling.

How to Play

Face your group and indicate the playing space. Say the following lines:

'This is our office, come into the office.'

'In the office we do two things – read…' (*Mime reading a book and encourage them to copy.*)

'…and type.' (*Mime typing and encourage them to copy.*)

'Who wants to be the boss?' Take a volunteer to be the boss and sit them on a chair with their back to the group. Instruct them to be as loud and 'bossy' as possible.

'If at any time the boss turns round and sees you not reading or typing, they will fire you.'

'Who wants to be late for work?' Choose a volunteer to be late and ask them to leave the room.

While they're out of the room, everyone else makes up an excuse for why they're late, e.g. 'My toaster exploded.' It's fine for the boss to be part of this discussion.

The employee comes in, positions themselves in front of the boss facing the rest of the group, and has to explain why they're late. Of course, they have no idea, so everyone else must mime the excuse behind the boss's back until the late employee has articulated it correctly. Encourage players to be as precise in their language as possible – 'my toaster broke' is not the same as 'my toaster exploded'.

However, if the boss turns round and catches anyone not 'working' (typing/reading), they will be fired and must leave the office. They can come and watch from behind the late employee.

Once your cast have got the hang of the game, ask them to suggest scenarios that relate to your play, e.g. 'Three witches told me I'd be king', 'A fairy turned me into a donkey', 'I was shipwrecked in a tempest'. Keep the excuses simple so that it's clear when the late employee has guessed correctly.

This game is great because being 'out' is almost as enjoyable as playing, the fired staff become an audience for the frantic attempts to convey the excuse.

Reflect with your cast on what makes for engaging storytelling, when meaning is clear, and the different tactics used to convey meaning without words.

You can return to this exercise throughout your rehearsal, increasing the complexity of the excuses as your company form a deeper understanding of the story.

The Aim of the Game

This playful exercise will energise your group and help them to understand the importance of clear storytelling in performance. It is a great warm-up for large groups as everyone is engaged all the time, even when they are 'out'. It also gives you a chance to explore some of the plotlines of the play in a light-hearted way.

Players	Age	Time
6+	8+	10
Characterisation, Imagination, Improvisation, Storytelling, Teamwork		

Can I Stay at Your House?

A quick warm-up that gets players thinking about character and interactions.

How to Play

You and your cast should start in the middle of the room. Ask your actors to move to a corner of the room – they can pick any corner.

Note how many people are in each corner, e.g. six, nine, three, five. Tell the cast that no matter what happens these corners should always have the same number of people in them, i.e. the corner with three people in it now should always have three people in it. That is the golden rule of the game.

When everyone is in their corners, approach each corner and demonstrate the following:

You say, 'Can I stay at your house?'

The group should respond, 'No, try next door.'

You then go 'next door' (to the next corner) and repeat the script, and so on.

At any moment a player could decide to 'move house' to a new corner. Everyone quickly swaps places to ensure that numbers remain consistent. You should take this opportunity to take a place in a corner as well, leaving someone new in the middle.

After you have played a few times you can start to introduce characters. The actor who asks the question 'Can I stay at your house?' chooses a style or character and the group has to mirror this in their response, e.g. if they ask in a Scottish accent, the group must respond in a Scottish accent; if they become a tall proud queen, or a withered witch, the group should do the same.

The Aim of the Game

This game is a playful way to introduce characters and the language of Shakespeare.

Players	Age	Time
10+	8+	10
Characterisation, Energy, Imagination, Voice		

PART TWO

STORY AND WORLD-BUILDING

'Thereby hangs a tale'
As You Like It

Above all else, Shakespeare was a master storyteller. I have had the privilege of watching someone discover this for the first time – the thrill of connection and the thump of emotion that come with experiencing a wonderful tale. This section will take you and your cast on the same journey of discovery.

The story of the play is the scaffold on which everything else is built. It is constructed from the events of the play, of course, but also from environments, characters and societies. These games explore all of this to help you and your actors to build a shared understanding and ownership of Shakespeare's stories. You will immerse yourself in the world of the play, imagining the sights, sounds, sensations and people that make the story possible. Stories are most effective when they are experienced, so we offer a variety of ways to make physical sense of the story using bodies and space, props and senses, imagination and collaboration.

Round Here We...

A collaborative way to make quick creative choices to define the world of the play.

How to Play

Set up some simple rules, beginning 'Round here we...' Your cast should bring them to life as you say them. Here are some suggestions to start the game:

- Round here we move around the space filling all the gaps when I say 'Go'.
- Round here we move like we have somewhere to be.
- Round here we acknowledge people when we pass them.
- Round here we all pause when I say 'Wait'.
- Round here we look at the audience when I say 'Audience'.

Next, layer in some rules of your own. They could be specific to your play, to a group of characters or your players, e.g.:

- Round here in *Macbeth* we're exploring a cold, spooky castle.
- Round here in *Richard III* we're very suspicious of each other.
- Round here in *Henry V* soldiers move in straight lines.
- Round here in Elsinore we bow when the queen enters.
- Round here in Verona we all love eating pizza.
- Round here in the forest the fairies take group selfies.

Once your company are responding enthusiastically and creatively, invite them to make suggestions in the same format: 'Round here we...' When a player makes a suggestion the rest of the company should bring their suggestion to life.

This is a good game to fire imaginations early in rehearsals and build the confidence of players in taking the lead and making suggestions. You and your cast can choose the rules that you like best to use again in future rehearsals. A few simple rules can be very helpful in building a consistent world where characters experience the same things. This is particularly useful when you need to set up contrasting worlds, e.g. Athens and the magic forest in *A Midsummer Night's Dream*, or contrasting groups of characters, e.g. Montagues and Capulets in *Romeo and Juliet*.

The Aim of the Game

This collaborative game will help you to create clear 'rules' for performance, and encourages your cast to take the lead in defining the world and characters of your play for the audience.

Players	Age	Time
5+	8+	15

Characterisation, Focus, Imagination, Improvisation, Teamwork

Ten Events

An introduction to the story arc and key plot points of the play.

How to Play

You can do this preparation alone or alongside your company, depending on their age and ability. (See the appendix on page 148 for instructions on how to produce the ten events for your play, and an example from CSSF for *Macbeth*.)

Divide your cast into groups and hand out one or two events to each of the groups, i.e. Group A gets events 1 and 2, Group B gets events 3 and 4, etc. Ask them to create a freeze-frame that represents the plot point they've been given. Give them about ten minutes to complete this task and challenge them to involve everyone in their group in the freeze-frame.

Ask each group to share their freeze-frames with everyone else. Run through these freeze-frames in order so that the cast can see their story come to life. Encourage an awareness of the audience: Where are they? Can all actors be seen? Ask the audience if they understand the picture and encourage participants to refine their freeze-frames to be as clear as possible. When everyone is satisfied you might find it helpful to take photos of freeze-frames to refer to throughout rehearsals.

Next, ask them to work in their groups to bring their freeze-frames to life for a few seconds. You could introduce some text at this stage and ask each group to incorporate a key line into their tableau.

Finally, instruct players to come up with an interesting transition from one event to another and run the whole thing from the beginning, including movement, Shakespeare's language and transitions. Point out to your cast that they have just staged the whole story of their play.

The Aim of the Game

This game will help your cast understand the story of their play. It should clarify the sequence of the plot for them and help them to refine their storytelling, as well as giving you a useful foundation for future rehearsals.

Variations and Extensions

Story Mountain

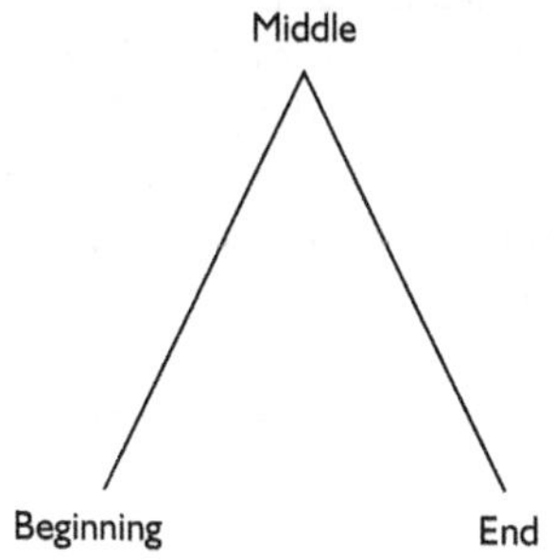

This is a simpler variation that will help you distil the story of the play to its essentials. First, read your cast a synopsis of the play. Draw a triangle structure like the one above and ask the following questions. We will use *Romeo and Juliet* as an example:

1. What is the world of the play like at the beginning? (e.g. unrest, conflict, warring families.)
2. What had changed by the end? (e.g. people have died, the two warring families are reconciled.)
3. What happened in the middle to create this transition? (e.g. there was a party, Romeo and Juliet got married, there was a fight.)

Decide on these key moments alone or with your cast. Once you have decided, ask them to create still images as above.

+ ten events on ten slips of paper		
Players	Age	Time
10+	10+	45–60
Comprehension, Imagination, Improvisation, Physicality, Storytelling, Teamwork		

Moodboarding

A collaborative, imaginative way to make choices about the world of your play.

Shakespeare's work continues to be produced because its universal characters and stories connect with actors and audiences in their own time. It can highlight truths about our own society and help us unravel the mysteries of the past. Directors therefore have a huge range of choices available on when and where their Shakespeare production is set. It is a good idea to play this game once your cast understand the story of the play and you are ready to decide *how* you want to tell that story.

How to Play

You may want to ask your cast to provide the pictures, music and objects for this game so that you can come to a collaborative understanding of the world of your play. Otherwise, bring an assortment of magazines, books, objects and musical instruments to the room. Variety is key – try not to have a closed idea of what is 'relevant' to your production. At this stage you are exploring ideas and discovering what resonates with your actors.

Put the pictures up on one wall of your rehearsal room and set up the objects on a table in a separate space. Ensure that there are plenty of each. In the centre of the room, place a large piece of paper.

Ask players to start in front of the picture wall. They should look at the pictures and decide which they are most drawn to based on the questions you ask them. Reassure them that they don't need to have answers for every question. Here are some suggested questions, you can add your own if you prefer:

- *Place* – What locations are in this play? They can be specific or more general – are there big open spaces? Interior spaces? Is it set in a specific country? Is it a place where lots of people go? Or is it a deserted place?

- *Time* – The play was written hundreds of years ago, but this doesn't mean this is when it has to be set. Do you want to set it then? Does the story lend itself to another historical period? Is it a modern setting? What time of year is it set? What time of day is it? How dark/light/warm/cold is it?
- *People* – Who is in the play? Individual characters but also what sort of people live in this world? Soldiers? Fairies? Families? Young people? Older people?
- *Mood* – What is the atmosphere of the play? Is it dark and gloomy? Or is it lighter and more hopeful? What does it feel like to be in this world?

Ask players to choose an image. It doesn't matter if several players choose the same image. Instruct them to stick them on the piece of paper in the middle of the room. This is your moodboard.

Now, bring the group to the table of objects. Tell them that they can touch and smell the objects as you are speaking, that you will be using your senses to imagine the environment of the play. This time your questions should focus on the sensory environment of the play – what can be seen, heard, tasted and smelt. In the world of the play…

- What colours are there?
- What shapes can you see? Are they straight? Curvy? Rough? Smooth?
- What can you hear? Are the sounds loud? Soft? Is it pleasant or not?
- What can you smell? Do you like the smell? Or do you dislike the smell?
- What can you taste in the air?
- What textures are there? Smooth and velvety? Rough and scratchy?

Players should choose the objects they were drawn to and bring them to the centre of the room with the moodboard.

Use your moodboard to inspire a discussion about the design of the play. Based on this moodboard, what kind of costumes might you wear? What about sound? Is there an instrument you want to feature?

Think of this as a creative journey to inspire you and your company. There are so many choices open to you in staging Shakespeare, and this exercise helps you to explore the different ideas of your company in a way that is rooted in the story and characters of your play. It doesn't matter if ideas are embryonic, or if they contradict each other. The next stage for you as a director is to organise those ideas – pick, choose, prioritise and develop into a coherent vision for your production.

The Aim of the Game

This exercise will help you and your company find a shared vision for your production. It uses all the senses to inspire ideas for the design of your show – the music, costumes and images that will make it your own unique production.

+ large pieces of paper, music, pictures, objects		
Players	**Age**	**Time**
2+	10+	30–60
Characterisation, Imagination, Storytelling, Teamwork		

See It, Be It

A game that encourages creativity and spontaneity.

How to Play

Ask your cast to move around the space and explain that, when you call out a number, they must quickly get into groups of that number. In these groups ask them to create shapes together, e.g. the largest shape they can make as a group, the smallest shape, the most twisted shape, the most jagged shape. Count down from ten and challenge them to do this without speaking, so that they have to watch and build on each other's ideas.

Next, ask groups to make pictures. Alternate instructions between 'seeing' something and 'being' something. Choose scenarios that are relevant to your play, particularly scenes with lots of people on stage, e.g. be a rowdy tavern, be a wedding, see a wedding, be soldiers returning from war, see a fight, be a fight. You may also like to suggest objects (e.g. be a fountain in Olivia's garden, be a blasted heath) or more abstract themes (be love, see love, be jealousy). Again, give them a count of ten to get into their picture and challenge them to create without talking.

Look at each other's pictures and discuss the difference between 'being' and 'seeing', and how important onstage reactions are for communicating a story. Identify what makes an interesting picture, and a believable reaction.

The Aim of the Game

Actors will be encouraged to both physicalise and visualise the world of their play, to use their bodies creatively on stage, and respond quickly and instinctively to direction. It highlights the importance of shared focus and reaction when characters are responding to something on stage, particularly something the audience can't see.

Players	Age	Time
5+	6+	20
Imagination, Improvisation, Physicality, Teamwork		

Character Cards

A quick way to introduce key characters and relationships.

How to Play

We will use the example of *Macbeth* but you should adapt for your play. This game will require some preparation and knowledge of the play.

Before you play, create character cards for your play and a summary of the story that includes these characters. (See the appendix on page 150 for instructions on how to produce these, and an example from CSSF.) It's up to you whether you make one for every character or just the key characters. Either way, all the characters should be mentioned when you come to read the story. Each card should have the character name and a brief description.

Split your company into small groups and give each group a character card. Ask them to make up an action for that character and a way to say their name inspired by the description on the card.

Bring players back into a circle. Go round the circle and ask each group to read out their character description, then do their action and say their name as a group. The whole group should repeat the name and gesture as a call-and-response.

You might like to take some characters, themes or locations and create them as a whole company, e.g. Scotland, Birnam Wood. You could split your characters according to where they belong or who they're related to (e.g. England or Scotland) and begin to create an understanding of the different worlds of your play.

Check understanding by asking quick comprehension questions, such as:

- Who is a supernatural character?
- Who has a son?
- Who is in the military?
- Whose name begins with M? Let's be clear who these different people are…

Now introduce the story. At CSSF we use our *Ten Events* summaries (see example on page 148).

The first time you read the story, ask participants to sit in a circle. Explain that, every time their character is mentioned, their group must stand up, do their action and say their name, then sit down again. You can adapt if you have players for whom standing up and sitting down is not available – instead all players could move forward slightly, or simply make sure the actions are performed with energy.

The second time, establish a playing space in the middle of the circle. Explain that you're going to read the story again but, this time, when they hear their character's name, groups should enter the playing space, do their action and say their name, then react and respond in character to the story being read. Encourage them to enter the space with pace, each character should aim to outdo the others with their energy and commitment to the story.

You can use the instruction 'clear the space' to reset the performance space between story points.

Challenge your cast by feeding characters a few short lines from the play – they should repeat these lines as they think the character would say them. It is important to layer this in gradually so that it doesn't feel overwhelming and Shakespeare's language is spoken in the room without any trouble.

The Aim of the Game

This is a very quick way of introducing a whole cast of characters, establishing relationships, exploring the entire story, delivering key lines and beginning to identify major themes. It also encourages full participation from everyone.

+ character cards, story of the play with key lines		
Players	**Age**	**Time**
10+	8+	30
Analysis, Characterisation, Imagination, Memory, Storytelling, Teamwork		

Story Bag

An inclusive way to explore the story using props.

How to Play

You will need to prepare a bag full of props related to your play. We will use the example of *Romeo and Juliet* here. You will also need a simple synopsis of the story of your play, incorporating key words to go with each object.

Ask your cast to get into a circle and explain that you will be telling the story of your play together and that there are some objects in the bag to help you. Pass the bag around the circle, asking players to pull out one object at a time and pass it on so that everyone can touch and experience it. You should choose objects that evoke the key themes and characters of your play. For *Romeo and Juliet* you could have, e.g.:

- A long red cloth to signify love – when this is pulled from the bag you would pass it all the way around the circle so that everyone is holding it, and explain that every time we hear the word 'love' we would pick up the cloth and make a heart shape together as a group. You could also choose a sound to signify love.
- A wooden dagger to signify death – although our story is about love, there is also killing and death in it. Every time the word 'kill' is mentioned, everyone could mime brandishing a dagger and repeat the word back in an aggressive tone.
- An Italian phrasebook to signify the setting of the story – in Verona, Italy. On hearing the word 'Verona', ask the group to take a step into the circle and to greet each other as though we're on the streets of the Italian city.
- A cap to represent Romeo. Ask a player to wear the hat and step into the circle. Everyone could say 'Hello Romeo' and wave, allowing Romeo to respond in whatever way they wish. Each time Romeo's name is mentioned, a different person could be given the hat and step into the circle.

- A sunhat to represent Juliet. As above, a different person could wear the hat and step into the circle each time her name is mentioned.

Before you read them the story, do a quick recap of your words, props and actions: 'Let's recap: It's a story about *love*, but people are *killed*. It's set in *Verona*, and it's about a boy called *Romeo* and a girl called *Juliet*.' Now, read your cast the story of the play, encouraging the actions every time the relevant words come up.

The Aim of the Game

This is a relaxed, inclusive way to introduce key characters, themes and plot points. It also encourages an ensemble approach to storytelling.

+ a bag filled with suitable props, synposis of play		
Players	Age	Time
5+	6+	30
Characterisation, Imagination, Memory, Storytelling, Teamwork		

Once There Was...

An exercise to help your cast understand the structure and sequence of the story.

How to Play

Like all stories, Shakespeare's plays follow a basic structure with a beginning, a catalyst, and then a series of events leading to the ending. Break this structure down for your cast as follows:

1. *Once there was... and every day...*
2. *One day...*
3. *Because of that...*
4. *Because of that...*
5. *Until finally...*

It is helpful to sketch this out on a flipchart or large piece of paper. Start with a well-known story, e.g. *Cinderella*. Ask your company to help you complete the sentences, e.g.:

> *Once there was...* a girl called Cinderella *and every day...* she was made to do terrible chores for her stepfamily.

This is the beginning, the 'Once Upon a Time' moment where we are introduced to the world of the play.

> *One day...* an invitation arrived at the house for a ball, hosted by the prince at his castle.

This is the catalyst – something that happens that breaks the norm and sets the rest of the plot in action.

A series of events needs to happen to allow the story to move on from the catalyst (the 'One day' moment) to the ending. Work with your company to identify these events for *Cinderella* – use the phrase '*Because of that...*' Keep it simple by only using three or four of these.

> *Until finally* the Prince discovered that it was Cinderella's glass slipper, they married and lived happily ever after.

This is the ending, in this case a 'happily ever after', where the reader or the audience knows the story has concluded. In Shakespeare, if it's a comedy, there is probably a wedding, and in a tragedy there is likely to be death!

Once you have done this for a well-known story, ask the cast to apply the structure to your play. Depending on the age and ability of your cast you may want to do this alone first so that you can confidently guide them. Start with the beginning, catalyst and ending (see the example below) and then fill in the middle afterwards. We have applied this structure to *Julius Caesar* as an example:

Once there was…and every day…

This is Act 1, Scene 1, line 1 – what are the normal lives of the characters before things begin happening?

Once there was a great leader called Julius Caesar *and every day* the people of Rome celebrated his victories and encouraged him to take more power.

One day…

What is the moment early on in the story when everything changes and sets the action in motion?

One day a group of senators, fearing that Caesar has become a dictator, plan how to bring about his downfall.

Jump forward now to…

Until finally…

What happens at the very end of the play?

Until finally, the conspirators die a noble Roman's death rather than suffer the disgrace of defeat.

Look back to your first point and notice how the world at the beginning of the play has changed to become the world at the end. You are going to fill in the gap in the middle with the things that had to happen to bring that change about. You can do this as a whole cast, or break them into smaller groups and come together at the end to agree.

Because of that… Because of that… Because of that…

Try to boil this down to three or four events. Remember, it's not about every detail, just your key events that follow logically from each other, e.g.:

Because of that Caesar arrives at the Capitol on the Ides of March and is assassinated.

Because of that Mark Antony speaks at Caesar's funeral and turns the mob against the conspirators, who flee the city.

Because of that Octavius joins forces with Antony to wage war on the conspirators.

When you have completed this exercise, you should have a 'flowchart' of the events that form the basic structure of your story. Now it's time to bring it to life!

Ask your cast to get into a circle. Read out the story that you have created together. When a new character is named, bring a player in to the circle to represent that character, responding to the story and reacting to other characters in the space. You could choose to feed in some key lines from the play at this point.

The Aim of the Game

This exercise will help you and your cast understand the narrative arc of your play, how each event drives the next, and what you need to emphasise in your performance.

+ flipchart or board, different-coloured markers		
Players	Age	Time
5+	10+	30
Analysis, Comprehension, Storytelling, Teamwork		

Tell It, See It, Map It

A sensory game to introduce the environment of the play.

How to Play

You will bring the environments of your story to life by creating a physical map of the world of your play. We will use the example of *Twelfth Night*.

1. Tell It

Read your cast a short, simple synopsis of the play. Once they have heard the story, ask them which words stand out and write up a list of them, e.g. shipwreck, twins, love, Viola, Illyria, Malvolio, stockings, fight. Make sure you include names, locations and events in your list. Next, ask the group to think of a gesture for each of these words. They could also add a sound. Retell the story, with the group adding in the gestures and sounds when they hear the relevant words. Now your cast understand the shape and characters of the story, you could encourage them to tell the story without you, using their words and gestures as scaffolding.

2. See It

Split your cast into groups and asked them to focus on the story's locations, e.g. one group could take the seashore after the storm, one group inside Orsino's court and another Olivia's house and garden. Ask them to think about a sensory way to evoke their location, e.g. bringing in trays of sand, handing round beautiful flowers to smell, sitting down to an imaginary dinner at Orsino's house. You could give your company the task to bring these sensory props to their next rehearsal, or provide an array of props for them to use in the moment. Each group should use these props to create their location in a specific part of the room.

3. Map It

Gather the company in the middle of the room and retell the story. Keep the sound and gesture responses but this time, every time a location is mentioned in the story, everyone should go to the part of the room where players have created that location, e.g. when you mention the seashore, the whole cast should move to the seashore location and explore it. Ask participants what it is like to be in that world and to consider how they move and respond to the various stimuli.

The Aim of the Game

This sensory approach will bring to life the different environments in the story and encourage the cast to immerse themselves in the world of their play.

+ story or synopsis of play, props and sensory items, pen and paper		
Players	Age	Time
5+	8+	60–120
Characterisation, Focus, Imagination, Memory, Teamwork		

PART THREE

INTRODUCING SHAKESPEARE'S LANGUAGE

'Stay, you imperfect speakers,
tell me more'
Macbeth

Shakespeare was the world's best wordsmith. He wrangled words to work for him, twisting and moulding them to create the most famous lines in literature. If a word didn't exist that expressed exactly what he wanted to say, or how he wanted to say it, he invented it. His language is descriptive, visceral, poetic and a lot of fun to say. Consider: dwindle, lacklustre, lonely, bump, zany or monumental. If you didn't know exactly what those words meant, would you be able to guess? We think so – and we take a similarly instinctive approach to Shakespeare in our games.

The games in this section deconstruct language just as Shakespeare himself did, and help players find their own way to the meaning of the words. They exploit the fun inherent in Shakespeare's writing, encouraging participants to experiment with the words and enjoy the way it feels to speak them. When meaning is uncovered through play and creative discovery, it sticks.

Double Double

A Macbeth*-inspired vocal warm-up.*

How to Play

This is a playful vocal warm-up. We have written it as a script for a group leader.

Ask the group to come into a circle and tell them that they are witches and they will be casting some spells.

'Before you begin your spells, you must travel to the spell circle. How do witches travel?' By broom. 'What noise does a flying broom make?' 'Broom broom' of course! (*A continuous humming, like a motorbike sound, blowing through closed lips.*)

Demonstrate it for your students. Encourage everyone to mount their invisible broom and make the noise. They must ride this broom up over mountains (the noise should become more high-pitched) and down under clouds (the noise becomes more low-pitched). They may need to swerve to avoid low-flying birds (they make some short sharp noises).

'Okay, you have arrived in the witch circle, welcome. You can get off your brooms. Imagine a cauldron bubbling away in the middle of the circle and prepare yourself to cast your spell. You do this by planting your feet firmly, hip-width apart, standing up straight and putting your arms by your sides.'

'To cast a spell you need a rhythm.' Teach this rhythm to the group: stamp left foot, stamp right foot, slap left knee, slap right knee, tap chest with left hand, tap chest with right hand, clap clap (this gives you eight beats).

When the group has got the hang of the rhythm, teach them the spell: 'Repeat after me, in time with our rhythm – "Double double toil and trouble / Fire burn and cauldron bubble."'

'Now, drop the actions, but keep that same vocal energy in casting your spell.'

'Now, focus on the sounds of the consonants in the line: D, B, T, N. Starting with D, I'd like you to fire "D" sounds like darts around the room – D D D D.'

Focus on D, B, T and N in turn.

To emphasise the consonants, add a flicking motion as they speak the line.

'Fantastic, let's make sure we're putting those strong consonant sounds into the line. It's time now to add our ingredients. As we chant the spell, throw ingredients into the cauldron with a flicking motion – make sure we are hitting each consonant.'

To elongate the vowels, add a stirring motion: 'Now we will stir the cauldron, let's stretch out the vowels as we stir the cauldron slowly with a big stick – "Doooouble doooouble tooooil and troooouble."' The stirring action should use their whole bodies.

'Fantastic, now we put both of those together (consonants and vowels) and deliver our line one final time into the cauldron to complete the spell.'

The Aim of the Game

This game will warm up faces and voices, and focuses on articulation in preparation for speaking Shakespeare's language. It's also a great way to introduce Shakespeare's use of rhythm.

Players	Age	Time
3+	6+	10
Imagination, Rhythm, Teamwork, Voice		

Diddly Dee

A game to get your cast used to communicating with unfamiliar language.

How to Play

Teach your cast this short rhyme:

'Diddly dee,
Diddly dee,
Diddly diddly diddly dee.'

When you are confident they've remembered it, ask them to get into pairs and label themselves A and B. They should say the rhyme between them, taking turns to say one word each:

A: Diddly

B: Dee

A: Diddly

B: Dee

A: Diddly

B: Diddly

A: Diddly

B: Dee.

Ask them to try to do this as quickly as possible, with energy and focus. Encourage and celebrate mistakes – this game is not about being word perfect, but rather embracing the fun of playing with language. These pairs can now move around the space whilst saying the rhyme to each other as if it is a conversation.

Next ask the group to get into fours. They now have to say the rhyme between all four of them. Each player can choose to direct their line to anyone else in the group. Ask them to think about what would make their decision easy to communicate, e.g. eye contact.

Now ask the four to move through the space and deliver the rhyme as before, as if it's a conversation. What characters emerge? What situations? You might like to invite the rest of the group to watch a few of these conversations. Ask them to notice what was engaging, what stories emerged, and how we in the audience could tell.

Reflect with your company – even though the words they are using do not have meaning, they have created meaning from them with their performance. The same will be true of their Shakespeare performance – the audience may not understand every single word, but they will understand the meaning through tone, gesture, movement, facial expression and reactions.

The Aim of the Game

This is a fun, energetic game that will help to break down concerns about speaking unfamiliar words, focusing on all the different ways we communicate meaning and intention on stage.

Players	Age	Time
8+	8+	15
Energy, Focus, Storytelling, Teamwork		

One-line Express

A great game to introduce Shakespeare's language.

How to Play

Hand out short lines of text from your Shakespeare play and instruct players to move around the space murmuring the line in order to get used to how the words feel in their mouths.

Ask the group to stop and deliver their line to a fixed point in the room. It can be useful to imagine they are sending the words down a line, so each word has to hit the final point with equal force.

Next, ask them to slow down the vowels in their lines and really emphasise them. Then they should highlight the consonants in a very fast and clipped way. Now ask them to emphasise both consonants and vowels.

Ask them to deliver the lines to different audiences, e.g. as though they are speaking to a sleeping baby in a cradle, then to someone at the very top of a mountain, and then to a friend next to them. Ask them to really imagine these people and reflect the scenario with their voices and bodies. Next, they should speak the lines in character, e.g. as if they are a terrible, hammy, Shakespearean actor and then as if they are a timid mouse. Now play with different intentions for the lines. Ask actors to speak them as though they are asking for more pocket money, or apologising to a parent, or as though they are telling a very important secret. This is about playing with the language, so encourage them to be exuberant and bold. You could also watch a few of your favourites back with the group.

Ask everyone to stop where they are and close their eyes. Tell them that you will move around the room and touch people on the shoulder. When you do so they should say their line out loud, however they like. Everyone else should listen and hear how the line sounds in the space. You will create a Shakespeare soundscape that should sound quite beautiful and interesting. Reflect with players about whether playing with the language like this uncovered any meaning for them.

You can use this exercise to begin exploring character through language, so be sure to reflect with players on how the different emphasis affects how the words sound, and how this might activate meaning about a character, e.g. 'What kind of character do you think would speak like this?', 'Does this way of speaking remind you of any other fictional/real characters?'

The Aim of the Game

For young actors a fear of getting it 'wrong' can inhibit their willingness to try. This exercise helps them to see that there is no single 'right' way to speak Shakespeare's words and to find their own way into the language. Encourage them to be playful and not to worry about the meaning of the lines initially.

Variations and Extensions

Circles of Attention

Often the most impactful choice an actor can make is simply being clear about who they are speaking to. This variation gives actors an opportunity to play with directing their line to different audiences. You can use the same lines as *One-line Express*, or even incorporate it into the game if you like.

Ask the group to imagine they are holding a candle in their hands, gently flickering. They should say their line to the candle. Reflect on what this does to their voice, and to their physicality. Were there any lines that this worked particularly well for?

Then ask players to choose one other person in the room and direct the line to them. How did this change their delivery? What about their bodies?

Next, ask them to deliver the line as if it is being said to every person in the room. What does this do to their focus? Does it change their movement or gestures? In what situation would a character speak like this?

Now, ask them to imagine that they are delivering the line to the elements, or the gods. What impact does this have on their voices and bodies?

Finally, ask them to choose a moment in the line where they change from one circle of attention to another, e.g. switch from speaking to the candle to speaking to the gods. Ask them to try a few different switches to see which works best for the line. What have they discovered about the meaning of the line? Watch a few of these with the rest of the group.

Reflect on which circle of attention suits which lines and why. You will be able to use this as a shorthand later in rehearsals if an actor is struggling to focus their lines.

+ lines of text written on pieces of paper		
Players 4+	**Age** 8+	**Time** 20
Analysis, Characterisation, Focus, Voice		

Tactics Circle

A game to develop and interpret character motivations and choices.

Every character in a Shakespeare play is trying to achieve an objective. These objectives are often specified in the text, e.g. in *A Midsummer Night's Dream*, Oberon tries to convince Titania to give him the changeling boy. His objective is to get the boy, but his tactics for achieving this objective are up to the actor portraying this character.

How to Play

Ask your actors to form a circle, placing one character (such as Titania in the example above) in the middle. The rest of the cast can now take turns to become Oberon and approach Titania with the line: 'Give me that boy.' Each time they move into the middle, they should adopt a different tactic to try to get what they want. You might like to give them a list to choose from, e.g.:

- Command Titania.
- Charm Titania.
- Shame Titania.
- Shock Titania.

You can refer to this game later in rehearsals if an actor is struggling to portray a particular emotion. Rather than saying 'Get angry when you say this line,' you could instruct Oberon to hurt or crush Titania.

The Aim of the Game

Encouraging actors to explore different tactics helps them find their own way to a unique interpretation of their character. Working as a group to discover what works on stage means that every member of the cast will develop a good understanding of the characters in their play.

Players	Age	Time
5+	10+	10
Characterisation, Comprehension, Storytelling, Teamwork		

One Word Add

A quick and playful way to access meaning in Shakespeare's dialogue.

How to Play

The instructions below are for duologues, but you could add this to *One-line Express* (game 23), with actors exploring a line individually.

Ask your cast to pair up and hand out a one- or two-line duologue. In their pairs, instruct them to cast themselves as the two characters and read through the duologue together once.

Next, the pairs should separate and everyone should find their own space in the room. They are going to move in straight lines so ensure they have space immediately in front of them.

Ask them to build their lines up, one word at a time, e.g.:

> Beseech
> Beseech you
> Beseech you, sir
> Beseech you, sir, be
> Beseech you, sir, be merry

They should take one step forward with each word. Each time they start the line again, they should change direction. Encourage players not to add a new word until they are happy with the words before – how they sound on their tongue, and what they might mean to their characters.

Give them enough time to reach the end of their lines and then ask them to come back into their pairs and repeat the duologue.

Reflect with them on how the exercise has affected their emphasis or intonation, and what they now understand about the meaning of the words. What have they discovered about their character from just this line? What worked or didn't work when they came back together in their pairs?

The Aim of the Game

In Shakespeare's plays, every single word is important. Young actors often forget this and rush lines without fully understanding their meaning. This exercise provides a playful way to help them build an understanding of meaning and character more slowly. It's also very helpful for line-learning!

+ a one- or two-line duologue		
Players	Age	Time
2+	10+	20
Characterisation, Comprehension, Rhythm		

Iambic Pentameter Made Easy

A clear, physical introduction to iambic pentameter.

How to Play

A line in iambic pentameter has ten syllables and creates a rhythmic pattern that sounds like this:

we STRESS the WORDS we WANT the WORLD to HEAR.

Ask students to tap this sentence like a heartbeat rhythm on their bodies – a light tap on the shoulder is followed by a firm one on the chest. Ask them if it reminds them of anything? Reflect that the rhythm is like a heartbeat beating through the text.

de-DUM, de-DUM, de-DUM, de-DUM, de-DUM.

As a group say this line in time with your tapped-out rhythm. Ask your students what they noticed, where does the heavy beat fall?

Present this line of text to your cast visually by arranging five participants into a line.

Quietly give two words to each participant and then get them to say them out loud down the line:

Student 1: We stress

Student 2: the words

Student 3: we want

Student 4: the world

Student 5: to hear.

Get them to stress the 'wrong' way first: Ask them to stamp their foot and stress their FIRST word and speak the second word normally. Reflect on how this sounds, and how it seems unnatural.

Next, create the 'right' (iambic) stresses: Repeat the line, this time stressing their second word. What do they notice? You will find that it sounds much more natural – the way the stress falls is the way we naturally speak in English. Notice also that the stressed words are the important ones – these are the words that carry the meaning and need to be clear to an audience.

Ask the line of players to only say the stressed words – you can get the sense of the line from this alone, e.g. 'Stress – words – want – world – hear'.

Try the same exercise with a Shakespearean line that fits the lambic pentameter, e.g. 'a HORSE, a HORSE, my KINGdom FOR a HORSE'. This should show your cast that Shakespeare's verse structures sound quite natural – the way that we would naturally stress the words in everyday speech is also the way that the poetic stress falls.

The Aim of the Game

The words 'iambic pentameter' strike fear into the hearts of many young actors (and adults too). This simple exercise will demystify the verse form, proving to your cast that it will actually help them decode and perform Shakespeare's texts.

Players	Age	Time
5+	10+	10
Comprehension, Focus, Rhythm		

Don't Stress, Just Stress

A game to help actors understand and make vocal choices.

How to Play

Begin with a line of modern English in iambic pentameter: 'I think I'd like another cup of tea.'

Tell players to get into pairs and choose a word to stress. Ask a few pairs to perform their line and discuss how the emphasis of the line shifts with each variation. A character who *thinks* they'd like another cup of tea might be indecisive. A character who thinks they'd like *another* cup of tea seems to be commenting on how much tea they're consuming. A character who thinks they'd like another *cup* of tea hates drinking tea in a mug, and so on.

It's likely also that students will choose different ways to stress the words – discuss the different effects produced. A character who bellows '*another*' is very different to a character who whispers it.

Now it's time for Shakespeare! Choose a speech (in verse) from your play and teach the first line to your whole company, e.g. 'Once more unto the breach, dear friends, once more' from *Henry V*.

Note that there are no right and wrong answers in this exercise, it is about choices:

Put players into pairs and ask each pair to choose:

- A word to stress or emphasise.
- A gesture for that word.
- A place for a pause.

The pairs should then find a way to deliver the line together, dividing it between them, e.g. 'Once more unto the breach / dear friends / once more.'

Ask pairs to perform their lines. Highlight the different choices, discussing the effect each one has on the meaning of the line and our interpretation of Henry as a character, e.g. emphasising 'once' might make Henry sound like he is pleading, while emphasising 'friends' might appeal to the camaraderie of soldiers.

Discuss other choices that affect emphasis besides stress and pause (you may have already heard some of the pairs doing them), e.g. speeding up/slowing down, raising/lowering volume.

Distribute all the lines of the speech amongst the pairs (i.e. a line or two per pair) and have them make choices (stress, gesture, pause) for the new lines. You might like to add in any other qualities discussed (e.g. a raising/lowering of tempo/volume).

Once they have decided on a version they like, have them practise delivering it as a pair (just like they did with first line). Line pairs up so that you have the whole speech represented and go through the whole thing. You may want to repeat it a couple of times to achieve fluidity. Discuss any particularly effective choices. If you have enough pairs for two or three versions, discuss the effect of the different deliveries.

It can be helpful to workshop lines or speeches in this way to give the actor speaking the speech lots of ideas to choose from. You may decide you would like to stage one of the major speeches using your whole cast, so that 'To be or not to be' becomes about the different voices in Hamlet's head, or 'Once more unto the breach' is taken up by Henry's whole army.

The Aim of the Game

This game is a good one to play after you have introduced your cast to iambic pentameter. Although the verse gives us a natural rhythm, actors still have a choice about which words to stress depending on their own interpretations of the character. This game demonstrates the wealth of possibilities for actors once they start using the vocal tools and opportunities the text makes available to them.

+ lines of a speech on strips of paper		
Players	Age	Time
4+	10+	30
Analysis, Characterisation, Rhythm, Teamwork, Voice		

PART FOUR

ACTIVATING SHAKESPEARE'S LANGUAGE

'Suit the action to the word,
the word to the action'
Hamlet

Shakespeare knew that the actors performing his plays did not have a lot of time to rehearse and develop their characters, so he used all the resources at his disposal to make their jobs easier. His language is littered with clues about character relationships, intentions, status and state of mind. These games put players in the role of detective, solving the clues and exploring the choices that Shakespeare laid out for them.

Learning does not happen in the mind alone, so we recommend taking an active approach to language – liberating actors from the script and connecting the words of Shakespeare with the movement of their bodies and the strength of their imaginations.

Mapping

A simple game to help comprehension and clarity.

How to Play

Choose a scene in which a few characters would be on stage and ask your actors to perform it. This can be done when they are familiar with their lines and off-book or reading from the text. Each time an actor mentions themselves (e.g. 'I', 'me', etc.), ask them to point to themselves. Each time an actor mentions another character (by name or through pronouns, e.g. 'thou', 'you', etc.), ask them to point to that character. Take care to ensure they're not missing any out and to go slowly if necessary.

Next, ask them to point every time they mention a place. As a company you will need to establish the geography of your play in relation to the stage in this scene, e.g. Where is the Capulet house from here? Which way is east? Which direction is the Friar? Where is heaven? Ask your actors to repeat the exercise and point to these locations.

Now, ask them to map any more abstract concepts in the text (e.g. 'love', 'death', 'soul'). Encourage them to make each concept as clear as possible.

Finally, ask your actors to run the scene again without the actor having to point every time. They should find ways to give the same emphasis, such as using other gestures, eye contact or vocal tone.

The Aim of the Game

In a Shakespeare play there are often many characters and their interweaving storylines on stage. This is a very simple exercise that will help your actors understand what, precisely, their character is talking about. It may also help with your blocking, as your actors learn to orient themselves in the world of the play.

+ a scene from your play		
Players	Age	Time
2+	8+	20
Characterisation, Comprehension, Focus		

Chair Swap

A physical exploration of how punctuation can uncover meaning in Shakespeare's language.

How to Play

Choose a soliloquy or speech with a lot of punctuation – e.g. Hamlet's 'To be, or not to be' – and ask one of your actors to read it.

Place two chairs a little apart from each other. In this task, the performer has to be sitting on a chair in order to speak, but must change chairs on every punctuation mark. The temptation is to 'cheat' by speaking as they move from one chair to another – encourage the performer to fully observe the rules of the exercise, and allow themselves the time they need to move from one chair to another without speaking.

Reflect with the performer and the rest of the cast on what they noticed. Did this change their understanding or delivery of the speech? Did they notice that one chair represented a certain train of thought and the other another? What did they notice about the pace of the soliloquy? How could they bring these discoveries in their final performance?

The Aim of the Game

Actors will find a lot of clues to the meaning of Shakespeare's text and the emotional state of his characters through the punctuation. Physicalising the punctuation in a long speech will help players break it down and make more sense of its meaning. It should also help them to slow down their delivery and pace the scene more carefully.

+ a speech from your play		
Players	**Age**	**Time**
1+	10+	20
Characterisation, Comprehension, Rhythm		

Punctuation Walk

An active way to explore the text for clues about character and intention.

How to Play

Choose a speech from your play. Ideally this would be a speech/soliloquy with a variety of punctuation throughout. A good example is this speech from *King Lear*:

> Rumble thy bellyful! Spit, fire! spout, rain!
> Nor rain, wind, thunder, fire, are my daughters:
> I tax not you, you elements, with unkindness;
> I never gave you kingdom, call'd you children,
> You owe me no subscription: then let fall
> Your horrible pleasure: here I stand, your slave,
> A poor, infirm, weak, and despised old man:
> But yet I call you servile ministers,
> That have with two pernicious daughters join'd
> Your high engender'd battles 'gainst a head
> So old and white as this. O! O! 'tis foul!

Ask your cast to read the speech aloud as they move around the room. When they reach the end of a sentence (a full stop, question or exclamation mark) they should turn their bodies 180 degrees and resume moving in the new direction. Reflect on what they discovered through this process. How often were they turning? How did that feel?

Repeat the exercise but now ask performers to also zig-zag on the commas, altering their direction by about 90 degrees.

Ask your players what they have discovered about the character at this moment in the play. Encourage observations on how their physical movements reflect the state of mind of the character, e.g. King Lear speaks in short sentences at the beginning when he exclaims at the storm. Later, his speech is more flowing, and he speaks a full two-and-a-half lines without any punctuation break as he raves on the subject of his daughters.

The Aim of the Game

It's thought that Shakespeare's actors did not have much time to rehearse and create their characters, so he put lots of clues about character and intention into his text. This exercise breaks down overwhelming chunks of text, clarifying a character's thought process and emotional journey.

+ a speech from your play		
Players	**Age**	**Time**
1+	10+	15
Characterisation, Comprehension, Voice		

Sentence Types

A physical way to explore sentence types in Shakespeare's text.

How to Play

You might like to combine this game with *Punctuation Walk* (game 30), which breaks a speech down into sentences.

Hand out a speech containing a variety of sentence types. Tell players that there are four main sentence types (below) and see if they can identify what they are from the speech you have given them.

Ask them to invent a movement or gesture for each sentence type. Alternatively, you can teach them the following:

- Exclamation – both hands punch the air.
- Question – shoulder shrug with palms facing the ceiling.
- Statement – both hands press down as if on a table in front of you.
- Command – point in a directive manner at the person/people you are speaking to.

Help players to learn these moves by playing a quick call-and-response game. Ask actors to move around the room and respond with the appropriate gesture when you call out the sentence type, e.g. You call out 'Question', and everyone shrugs. You could add a sound to each gesture to make it more dynamic.

Now return to the speech. Ask players to find their own space in the room and read the speech aloud, doing the appropriate gesture at the end of each sentence (they can lose the accompanying sound at this stage). They should not gesture throughout the sentence but rather land on their gesture as they conclude their sentence, e.g. the following speech spoken by Juliet:

> O Romeo! (*Exclamation: punch the air.*)
> Romeo! (*Exclamation: punch the air.*)
> Wherefore art thou Romeo? (*Question: shrug.*)

Deny thy father and refuse thy name.
(*Command: point.*)
Or if thou wilt not, be but sworn my love
And I'll no longer be a Capulet. (*Statement: press down.*)

Reflect with the cast on what they noticed as they did this exercise. What do the sentence types tell them about Juliet? (e.g. she is excited and determined.)

Sentence types are a short cut to information about a character's state of mind. They are also very useful for decoding status and relationships, e.g. if one character is always commanding another, they are probably a higher-status character (or think they are!), e.g. Lady Macbeth and Macbeth during the banquet scene, he might be King but she is the one with most of the 'command' sentence types. We recommend you try this game with a duologue to demonstrate this.

The Aim of the Game

Shakespeare's texts give actors lots of clues about their characters' personalities, status and relationships. This game is a good introduction to unpicking these clues. Physicalising sentence types will also add energy and intention to actors' lines.

+ a speech from your play		
Players	**Age**	**Time**
1+	8+	20
Characterisation, Comprehension, Focus		

Antithesis

A couple of games to demonstrate the importance of antithesis in Shakespeare's language.

Shakespeare's stories are full of conflicts – characters in conflict with one another as well as characters in conflict with themselves, e.g. Juliet deciding to marry her family's sworn enemy. Shakespeare used antithesis to highlight the oppositions at the heart of his stories. These games will help your cast spot antithesis, understand its importance, and learn to flag it up for their audience.

Echo, Echo

Take a section of text that contains a set of oppositions you wish to explore. Give these oppositions a heading, e.g. with Juliet's 'O serpent heart, hid with a flowering face' speech, the two headings might be 'positive' and 'negative'.

In other speeches, the oppositions will be more specific, e.g. for Philo's speech at the beginning of *Antony and Cleopatra*, you could listen out for anything to do with women/sex versus war/fighting; when Claudio jilts Hero at the altar in *Much Ado*, you could listen out for anything to do with exterior/appearance/show versus interior/truth/reality.

Allocate an actor or actors to read the piece, and split the rest of the group into two halves, one for each heading. Instruct each half to listen out for words, phrases or associations which fall under their heading.

Now, ask your actors to read the text aloud, while the two halves echo in a whisper anything they hear to do with their heading. The group doesn't have to echo in unison: everyone will respond differently, at different times. The aim is not to reach consensus, but to explore the full range of possibilities of where the oppositions might be.

Polar Opposites

This is a variation on the game that works for just one actor.

Choose two different points in the room. This could be two chairs, or two walls. Agree which point represents which opposition, e.g. in Hamlet's famous soliloquy one chair is 'to be' (to live) and one 'not to be' (death).

Ask the actor to move between the two points depending on what they are saying or thinking. At first, say that they must be touching one of the two points in order to speak. This will also help them to pace their soliloquy. They may then discover that the character wants to be between the two at some points in the speech. In the next version, therefore, they can move anywhere on a sliding scale between the two points. Ask them to make conscious choice at every punctuation mark.

Reflect with your cast on how the antithesis helps define the character's meaning and discuss how they can demonstrate this for their audience.

The Aim of the Games

These games will demonstrate to your cast the prevalence and importance of antithesis in Shakespeare's texts, helping them to communicate it to their audience.

+ a speech from your play containing antithesis		
Players	Age	Time
10+	10+	15
Characterisation, Comprehension, Focus, Voice		

Most Rare Vision

An exercise for decoding, visualising and enjoying Shakespeare's language.

In the opening speech of *Henry V*, the chorus says, 'Think when we talk of horses that you see them.' Shakespeare asks his audience to collaborate in the storytelling process by picturing the world of the play. In characters' speeches he conjures fantastical and incredible images that would be impossible to stage, and which the audience must imagine. This game will help players unpick and enjoy this imagery and form their own connection to Shakespeare's beautiful language.

How to Play

We will use Calpurnia's vivid description of her prophetic dream in *Julius Caesar* as an example:

> A lioness hath whelped the streets;
> And graves have yawn'd, and yielded up their dead;
> Fierce fiery warriors fought upon the clouds,
> In ranks and squadrons and right form of war,
> Which drizzled blood upon the Capitol;
> The noise of battle hurtled in the air,
> Horses did neigh, and dying men did groan,
> And ghosts did shriek and squeal about the streets.

Choose a speech with similarly vivid imagery or use this one. Put players into pairs and name them A and B. Ask them to find their own space in the room and sit down together. Give each pair a copy of the text.

Ask As to close their eyes. B should read the speech slowly to their partner, one image or little chunk at a time. After hearing each chunk, A should allow an image to form in their mind. They shouldn't censor themselves – this is about their own imaginations, there is no 'right' answer. Once they can see the image, they should nod once to tell B to read the next chunk. If B needs to repeat the phrase before A nods, that's alright. Move in this way through the whole speech.

Tell A to describe to B some of the most memorable images that they saw – prompt them to go into detail about tastes, sounds, colours, smells, etc. Discuss as a group the images that were especially vivid for people. Were certain words particularly rich? How did the pictures in people's heads differ?

You will find that certain phrases are particularly evocative, e.g. the yawning graves and drizzling blood. Discuss why this is – what is Shakespeare tapping into? You will also find that people conjure very different images from the same words, because the bank of reference in everyone's brain is different. This is to be celebrated – your actors now have a unique connection to the text.

Swap over so A is reading to B.

Reflect with your cast on their experience as listeners. What was it in the delivery (tone of voice, pauses, etc.) that produced rich images? What was it in the beautiful language? This game should demonstrate that it is the combination of Shakespeare's wonderful language and the choices of an actor that make a story work for an audience.

If your players enjoyed this game you might like to continue it by asking them to draw pictures or make freeze-frames of the images that were generated for them.

The Aim of the Game

This game demonstrates Shakespeare's timeless capacity to excite our imaginations. It will give players a deeper understanding of and personal connection to the text.

+ a speech with vivid imagery		
Players	**Age**	**Time**
2+	10+	20
Comprehension, Focus, Imagination		

Image-Makers

A game to help actors engage with Shakespeare's rich imagery.

Shakespeare's work was originally performed without elaborate sets, meaning his audiences had to use their imaginations to conjure the world of the play. Shakespeare's texts are full of vivid descriptions to help us imagine where they are taking place, but also to picture the characters' internal worlds – their emotions, opinions and reactions. We will use the opening of *Richard III* as a good example. On the one hand we have the depiction of war as a 'winter of discontent… grim-visaged… wrinkled', etc.; on the other, peace is 'sun… smooth'd… capers… lascivious'.

How to Play

Choose a speech that is rich in imagery from your own play, or use the opening of *Richard III* below:

> Now is the winter of our discontent
> Made glorious summer by this sun of York;
> And all the clouds that lour'd upon our house
> In the deep bosom of the ocean buried.
> Now are our brows bound with victorious
> wreaths;
> Our bruised arms hung up for monuments;
> Our stern alarums changed to merry meetings,
> Our dreadful marches to delightful measures.
> Grim-visaged war hath smooth'd his wrinkled
> front;
> And now, instead of mounting barbed steeds
> To fright the souls of fearful adversaries,
> He capers nimbly in a lady's chamber
> To the lascivious pleasing of a lute.

As a group, read the whole speech through, or you might like to ask the group to close their eyes and read it to them. Encourage players to form pictures in their minds as you do so.

Give the speech to an actor and ask for some volunteers to be their image-makers. The rest of the cast should form an active audience. The actor reads the speech out loud, slowly. As they are reading, the other actors form images around them, e.g. in the *Richard III* introduction you might ask an actor or group to form the peace images and another to form the war images. If actors are stuck, they can ask the audience for help.

The speaking actor reads again. This time, they should find a way to be in the pictures themselves, interact with the image-makers or directing them, e.g. Richard might huddle, shivering with the war/winter images and caper happily with the peace/summer images. They should take their time, not progressing with the speech until they're happy with the images.

Finally, remove the images. The actor reads the speech but imagines they are still there. This can take many forms, from mapping them out for the audience to reacting with a facial expression. Either way, this actor suddenly becomes an amazing storyteller.

Take your time with this exercise. The text is dense with imagery and exploring one speech in this way will open your company's eyes to the richness of the whole text.

The Aim of the Game

This game will help your actors make sense of Shakespeare's rich, visceral language and take ownership of it. It should also encourage them to slow down the delivery of important speeches, and enjoy the sound and feel of the words.

+ a speech with vivid imagery		
Players	Age	Time
3+	10+	30
Comprehension, Focus, Imagination, Physicality, Storytelling		

Ghosting

A simple technique to access the meaning of Shakespeare's texts.

How to Play

Hand out a scene and ask for volunteers to be the characters. Duologues work well to introduce this technique.

Now take away their scripts and give them each a 'ghost' assistant to feed them their lines. There are four stages to *Ghosting*:

1. *Line Repeat* – Instruct your ghosts to feed the actors their lines. They must be audible, neutral and break the text down into bite-sized chunks. The actors have to listen to the line, decide who they are speaking to, and then deliver it with intention. Encourage them to make connections with the speech and move in the space if this feels natural to them. The ghosts will follow if they move.
2. *Own Words* – After they have tried this with Shakespeare's text, ask your characters to try expressing the lines in their own words. The ghost will feed them in Shakespeare's language, as before, but the actor finds their own words to convey the meaning. If Shakespeare's original line makes perfect sense, the actor doesn't have to change it. If your actors get stuck at any point, they can ask the rest of the group to help.
3. *Improvise* – Ask the actors to do the scene in their own language again but without the ghosts, improvising as much of the content of the scene as possible. Encourage them to be bold with their choices.
4. *Shakespeare* – Reintroduce the ghosts and return to Shakespeare's text. Ask the actors to try to retain any moments they liked, or that the audience identified as engaging when the actors were playing it in their own language.

This is a great technique to return to whenever you see your actors struggling with the meaning of a piece of text.

The Aim of the Game

Often when you give young actors a script to read from, all sense of play goes out of the window. Even for good readers it feels like a test and they tend to cling to the page and lose the physicality of their performance. Ghosting liberates the actor from the page, encouraging actors to find their own understanding of the text. It is also a fantastic way of learning lines.

+ a scene from your play		
Players	Age	Time
2+	8+	20–30
Characterisation, Comprehension, Focus		

This is for You

A game to introduce character intentions.

How to Play

Ask the group to get into pairs, and teach them the following exchange:

A: This is for you.

B: For me?

A: For you.

B: Thank you.

Introduce an object into the exchange, so that one character is giving away the object and the other character takes it.

Ask your players to think about different ways that they could deliver the line and how this changes the way they give or take the object. What happens if they don't want their partner to have the object? What happens if they really want to give it away? How does one actor's delivery affect the reaction of their partner?

They should see that their performance is about more than the delivery of their lines as written. This simple exchange can be performed in thousands of ways, depending on the intentions of the actors delivering it. Watch a few exchanges to illustrate this point.

The Aim of the Game

The language in Shakespeare's plays is very active, i.e. characters speak because they want to achieve something with their words. This game is a good way to introduce the concept of character intentions to your cast.

Variations and Extensions

Pass the Object

You can then use this notion of passing intention through the object and apply it to a scene you are working on. This is especially useful for dialogue with more than two characters, e.g. Brutus, Cassius and the conspirators discussing Caesar's assassination.

An actor must be holding the object each time they speak a line. You could start by having the characters take the object from the opposite party whenever they begin to speak.

Try again, this time with the characters giving the object at the end of their lines.

Finally, allow the actors to choose whether to give or to take the object, exploring how the impetus changes at different moments. Ask your company to consider how the intention with which they give or take the object affects the stories and characters that they are portraying, e.g. Why does Cassius hesitate to take the object here? Why is Brutus so keen to get hold of it in this moment?

At this point you can then remove the object and ask your actors to repeat the scene, keeping all of the focus and intention they discovered when passing the object.

+ objects and a scene from your play		
Players	**Age**	**Time**
2+	8+	15–20
Characterisation, Comprehension, Focus, Teamwork		

Yes It Is, No It Isn't

A game to inject Shakespeare's language with intention.

How to Play

Ask your cast to get into pairs and label themselves A and B. Give the line 'Yes it is' to the As, and the line 'No it isn't' to the Bs. Tell them that they only have this single line to win an argument. Encourage them to really persuade their partner, rather than shouting them down.

After thirty seconds, pause the group and raise the stakes, e.g. you could say 'Imagine that whoever loses the argument will have to repeat their year at school.' Again encourage them to listen and respond to each other and then give them a countdown – they have twenty seconds to win the argument…

Watch some arguments back and reflect with the group about how everyone had one objective but tried different tactics. What were those tactics? Did they threaten, cajole, entice, demand? Try to progress from observations about body language and vocal tone ('they shouted', 'they walked away') to focus on intention – what were they trying to do to the other character? You could then start a discussion about the different tactics that the characters in your play use at different points.

Now you can bring Shakespeare's language back. Choose a line from your play and give it to A. The meaning of the line isn't important, but it should be short and memorable. A must use this line to calm their partner. Encourage Bs to be genuinely upset so that As have to work really hard to calm them down. If one tactic isn't working, they should try another. Encourage them to move around the space if that feels natural. Watch a few pairs, and discuss with the group the different ways As were choosing to calm their partner.

Now swap over, and ask Bs to use the same line to belittle As. Again, spotlight a few and reflect on the different ways that Bs were belittling their partners.

It doesn't matter if the line doesn't make sense with this intention, your actors should find that they can express their intentions regardless.

Remind them that these are all things they want to do to the person they're speaking to. They shouldn't act 'shocked' or 'threatened'.

Now ask them to apply this to a section of the scene and try to identify the actions that most suit their characters. In every scene it is vital that the actor knows why they are there – and what they want to achieve. This game may help them discover this intention for themselves.

The Aim of the Game

Young people can be very intuitive about the best way to get what they want, but often when you put them on stage they forget their instincts. This can be particularly true when faced with the unfamiliar language of Shakespeare. This exercise will help them realise and explore the tactics that they can use to achieve their objective on stage, expressing their intentions through gesture, movement and vocal quality to tell a clear story.

Variations and Extensions

Try with physical rather than psychological actions, e.g. punch, flick, wring, stroke or squeeze (see *Punching the Line*, game 38).

To make this as playful and experimental as possible, you may want to put different actions in a hat and have players pick them out, or write them on paper stuck up in different parts of the room and have players switch tactics as they move around the space.

+ a scene from your play		
Players	**Age**	**Time**
2+	8+	20
Characterisation, Energy, Focus, Storytelling, Voice		

Punching the Line

A game to add emotion and intention to voice.

How to Play

This exercise works well in a circle or with the cast spread around the room. Ask your cast to pick one of their lines from the play or choose one that everyone can work on together. Choose a line that packs an emotional punch and which could be delivered in several different ways, e.g. 'A plague on both your houses.'

Tell them that they will be saying the line out loud, and you are going to give them a physical action to perform as they do. They should allow the action to affect their voice and the way they say the line. Some suggested actions are below, adapted from the 'efforts' devised by influential twentieth-century dancer and theorist Rudolf von Laban.

- Punch – imagine a punchbag in front of you and punch it.
- Wring – imagine you are holding a big wet towel and squeezing all the water out of it.
- Stroke – imagine you are in front of a long velvet curtain, and you are gently stroking it.
- Flick – imagine you are flicking water off your wet hands.
- Squeeze – imagine you are squeezing a big stress ball.

Now ask players to repeat the line without the action, keeping the same vocal quality. Push them to commit – use scaling if helpful. As a cast, watch a few of these lines being delivered. What do they notice? Do certain actions suit certain lines? How has the actor's vocal performance changed? What has it done to the character at that moment?

Players should notice a significant difference and you will now have a shared language to use later in rehearsals, e.g. during Lady Macbeth's 'Out, damn spot' speech, you could ask, 'What would happen if you tried to "wring" these words?' Instructions like this are usually more helpful than asking an actor to speak with 'more emotion'.

The Aim of the Game

Shakespeare's characters experience extraordinary events and intense emotional journeys – they feel love, rage, awe and fear in a way that young actors have probably not encountered personally. This game is a fun way to help actors inject emotion into their voices. It will also give you a shared language to use later in rehearsals when needed.

Players	Age	Time
2+	10+	30

Characterisation, Improvisation, Storytelling

Improv Layers

A layered improvisation game to find character intention in the text.

How to Play

Choose a scene where characters have a strong 'want'. Scenes with two characters in opposition work well if you are trying this for the first time, e.g. Oberon and Titania, Richard and Lady Anne. Tell the rest of your cast that they will be an active audience. You might want to read through the scene once with the group, checking comprehension and unpicking any unfamiliar words. Tell the actors that they are trying to 'win' the scene by achieving their intention. At each stage identify with the actors and audience the moments that were successful in revealing more about the characters.

1. No Words

Ask each of your actors to think about their character's reason for being on stage and how they want to change someone else, e.g. Richard III wants Lady Anne to agree to marry him, Lady Anne wants him to leave her alone. Once the actors have identified their objective, ask them to enter the scene, and reduce that intention to a physical demonstration – a stance, gesture or look. They should think clearly about what their intention is and show that thought to the audience without speaking. Ask your audience if they knew what the characters wanted? Why? Could they be clearer? How?

2. One Phrase

Ask the actors to reduce their intentions to one phrase. This should be in modern language and something that they would say, e.g. when Richard III is trying to woo Lady Anne, he might say 'Marry me,' whilst Anne might say 'Go away.' If they are struggling to come up with a line, you can turn to the rest of your company for help.

Once they are happy with their phrase, ask your actors to enter the space and try to 'win' the scene using only that phrase. Encourage the actors to keep the stakes high and ensure that they are responding to each other, not just repeating the phrase in the same way.

3. Modern Language

Tell your actors to keep these core intentions in mind and return to the start of the scene. This time they can do or say anything in modern language that will help them achieve what they want from the scene. They are playing the scene, from memory, in their own words. It doesn't matter if they forget the exact sequence of events, what's important is strong intention and genuine reaction. Encourage them to use different tactics and remind them that they can always go back to the one phrase if they are struggling to come up with something to say.

4. Back to Shakespeare

It is time to return to Shakespeare's language. Ask your actors to play the scene as scripted but to remember all of the intentions and actions that they discovered so far. At this stage, actors often lose all of the brilliant instinctive choices they've found in the improvisation. If you see this happening, encourage them to use their one phrase to help them rediscover their motivation.

We encourage you to run these layers in whatever order suits your performers' needs, returning to different layers as and when you need to.

The Aim of the Game

This layered game will help your actors tap into their instincts, make choices about the intention and core motivation of their characters, and perform them in a clear and compelling way. Working with an active audience will create a sense of shared ownership and collaboration in your cast.

+ a scene from your play		
Players	**Age**	**Time**
2+	10+	20–30
Characterisation, Imagination, Improvisation, Teamwork		

Barriers and Posse

An ensemble game to add energy and pace to onstage arguments.

These two games are perfect for scenes between two characters who are sparring. We have used the example of Beatrice and Benedick here.

Barriers

Set your two characters at opposite ends of the room. Divide the rest of the company into two, and ask them to form two lines with arms linked, one line in front of each of the characters.

The two speaking actors play the scene, but their task is to try to physically reach their opponent as they speak – by leaning over, crawling under, and pushing through the line.

Ask your actors how this made them feel, and what it did to their voices when they had to work in this way. Ask them to repeat the scene but take away the physical blocks, encouraging them to retain the intensity in their body and voice.

Depending on your cast, you can vary the degree of physical obstacle/challenge in this game, e.g. you could set the speaking characters the same challenge of getting to each other, but no physical contact is allowed – the ensemble move around and in-between them like a fluid barrier.

Posse

Set your two speaking characters facing each other across the room. Divide the rest of the group into two and give each character a 'posse' or crew. The posse will try to help their leader to 'win' the battle. They will do this by using voice and gesture to intimidate and belittle their opponent, while supporting their leader, e.g. when Beatrice speaks, her posse will agree with all her points and when Benedick speaks, Beatrice's posse will hiss or boo, and vice versa.

The characters speaking the text will have to compete with all the noise. Not only will they have to work at a more energised physical and vocal level, but they will not feel as exposed as when they are performing alone in a quiet room.

You may choose to leave the posse in your final production, but even if you remove them this game should improve the energy and pace of the speaking actors.

The Aim of the Games

Shakespeare's characters are often in conflict, and these scenes can be tricky for young actors as they require an intensity of emotion that can make them feel vulnerable. These simple games help overcome this, bringing energy, pace and intention to argument scenes. They are great games for involving the whole cast in a scene with only two speaking characters, and should help everyone clarify their understanding of the characters and stories – the posse will have to listen to their leader in order to know when to chime in.

Variations and Extensions

Ask the ensemble to 'vote with their feet' and switch sides according to who they feel is more convincing. This works well in crowd persuasion scenes, e.g. Brutus's and Antony's speeches at Caesar's funeral.

+ a scene from your play		
Players	**Age**	**Time**
10+	8+	15
Characterisation, Energy, Physicality, Teamwork, Voice		

Last Word Repeat

A game to develop listening skills and onstage reactions.

How to Play

You can do this exercise with your whole cast, working in pairs, or with two characters in dialogue.

Choose a scene with two characters in conversation, e.g. Macbeth and Lady Macbeth.

Each performer repeats the last word of what the other character has said to them before saying their own line, e.g.:

> LADY MACBETH: He has almost supped. Why have you left the chamber?
>
> MACBETH: Chamber. Hath he asked for me?
>
> LADY MACBETH: Me. Know you not he has?

Encourage the actors to keep eye contact with the other character while listening and repeating. If still on-book, they should only look at their script while speaking their own lines, and not at any other time.

Once the performers have got to grips with this, you can develop the exercise by loosening the rules. Instead of repeating just the last word, the performers can repeat a couple of words or a phrase if it makes more sense. They should also change pronouns if necessary to make grammatical sense. They should think about how to use the repeated words to launch their own line, e.g. do they become questions?

> LADY MACBETH: He has almost supped. Why have you left the chamber?
>
> MACBETH: The chamber? Hath he asked for me?
>
> LADY MACBETH: Asked for you? Know you not he has?

Finally, ask your actors to repeat the last few words in their head rather than out loud. Play the scene again with your actors repeating the line in their heads, but if there are any particular phrases they want to repeat out loud then encourage them to keep these in – what does this do to the scene?

Ask your cast to think about how this repetition (both external and internal) informs the scene and develops the relationships between the characters. It may be helpful for the rest of the cast to watch two actors do this exercise so they can see the impact it has.

The Aim of the Game

A large part of acting is reacting to other characters on stage. This is something that younger actors often struggle with – if they are not speaking they sometimes think they are not acting. This game dispels that notion and acts as an instant reaction generator, helping them to listen and respond to each other.

Variations and Extensions

Actors can repeat any phrases that provoke a reaction, even if they don't speak next. This is particularly useful in scenes with a 'crowd' of non-speaking characters (parties, weddings, big court scenes, etc.). Rather than always repeating the last few words of a line, ask actors to listen out for any phrases that prompt a reaction from their character and repeat those. Sometimes everyone may repeat one line ('Heat of a luxurious bed?!'), sometimes there will be variety between bystanders. The next stage is to choose which reactions to keep out loud, and which you would prefer actors to represent without speaking.

+ a scene from your play		
Players	**Age**	**Time**
2	10+	15
Characterisation, Comprehension, Teamwork		

PART FIVE

CHARACTER

'O brave new world,
that has such people in't'
The Tempest

Even Shakespeare's most otherworldly characters are rooted in the human experience – Caliban is a monster who rails against the hardship of serving an unjust master; Titania and Oberon are fairy royalty that argue like any married couple; Hamlet is a grieving boy who can see ghosts. These games help actors make a human connection with their characters, exploring motivations and relationships, circumstances and emotions. Every character matters, and many of these games will drive that point home, helping you to build an ensemble who are all equally invested in telling their story.

We take a kinaesthetic approach with fun, active games that help players develop interesting, believable characters from the outside in. The games will illustrate the choices that actors have and help you to create performances that work as well for the audience as they do for the players.

Mystery Party Guest

A fun improvisation game to help actors get into character.

How to Play

Tell your cast that they are going to a party. Ask them what they do at a party and take some suggestions, e.g. have drinks, dance, eat, chat to friends, play games. Now tell them that on the count of three you want them to turn the rehearsal room into a brilliant party. Let that play out for a few seconds and congratulate them on their work.

Divide the group in half. One half of the group will stay in the room and continue to enjoy the 'party' – they don't have to stick to one action, they can just move around as they would if they were at a real party. The other half will leave the room and enter the party, one by one, in character as someone from a Shakespeare play. They can choose any character they like – they should not tell the others their choice and it doesn't matter if several people choose the same character. Tell players to think about what their character might say and do on entering a party.

When they are ready, the first person should knock on the door, enter and greet the other guests. Give them about ten seconds to improvise their character's behaviour at a party, e.g. Malvolio may start to serve drinks to others, but in a very haughty and imperious manner; Lady Macbeth may start to behave as though she is the hostess and go around graciously greeting guests (while staring murderously behind their backs). The group in the room have three guesses as to which character it is. If they are stumped, they could ask the actor to perform a specific action in character, e.g. could you pour yourself a drink in character?

Once they have guessed correctly, the actor should stay at the party in character. The next actor to enter the room does the same thing but can also interact with the first character. The game continues until everyone is in the room.

Swap the groups over so that everyone has a chance to enter in character.

The Aim of the Game

Shakespeare wrote some of the most iconic and recognisable characters in literature. This game is a playful, low-stakes way for the actors to engage with these characters and identify their defining characteristics, honing their body language and mannerisms.

Variations and Extensions

If players are nervous about being the centre of attention, you could try asking actors to get into pairs and agree a character between them. They would then enter the room together, both in character.

Alternatively, all the guests at the party could mirror the character coming in – not copy exactly what they are doing but take on the vocal quality and characteristics, e.g. Iago comes in and greets everyone in a shifty manner, everyone in the room will become shifty.

Players	Age	Time
8+	10+	30

Characterisation, Imagination, Improvisation, Teamwork

Archetypes

A physical way into creating a unique character.

How to Play

Archetypes are bold character types that appear in stories across history, cultures and genres. Introduce your cast to the following archetypes and discuss which characters they might apply to. Ask everyone to find their own space in the room and follow your instructions with their bodies. Encourage them to experience the archetype in the biggest way possible. You can then introduce a 1-to-10 scale if you need them to tone it down.

- *The Innocent* – The Innocent has their feet parallel and their weight slightly forward on the balls of the feet. The Innocent knows nothing and learns nothing. The Innocent is always moving into new space and every experience they have feels like their first. They move in a light way. Their eyes are wide, e.g. Romeo, Ophelia, Miranda, Lear's Fool.
- *The Champion* – The Champion is strong and proud, with an open chest and face. They are always on a quest for something other than personal gain. The Champion has superhero energy. Nothing is thought about or considered; the Champion sees, and then does. They work in straight lines and are direct and definite, e.g. Henry V, Lysander, Rosalind, Juliet.
- *The Carer* – The Carer is always ready to embrace and welcome. They have an open stance, feet slightly wider than hip-width apart, toes turned out, arms open wide. Their head is slightly angled, their eyes are soft. The Carer nurtures and tends to others. They exude warmth. They move calmly and with confidence, e.g. The Nurse, Prospero, Titania.
- *The Trickster* – The Trickster is like a crab, always side-on or concealing themselves. They don't like you to look in to their eyes and always close their body physically, turning away from others. The Trickster will approach everything tactically, for personal gain, e.g. Puck, Mercutio, Regan, Iago.

- *The Monarch* – The Monarch is straight and tall. They tend to move the whole body when they move their head. They do very little; they don't need to – they are in charge. They have the highest-possible status, e.g. Lear, Titania, Lady Macbeth, Malvolio.

Most characters are a combination of archetypes so try to experiment with some combinations. As a director, you will find the language of archetypes useful at key moments, e.g. ask the actor playing Demetrius to change suddenly from a Trickster to a Champion the moment Puck drips the flower's love potion onto his eyes.

The Aim of the Game

This game will encourage actors to embrace a larger-than-life stage physicality and to understand the driving energy of their characters. It will give you a shared language to use later in rehearsals.

Variations and Extensions

- Ask each actor to choose their favourite archetype and move around the space. Experiment with what happens when different archetypes meet one another.
- Write the name of each archetype on a piece of paper and place them in different parts of the room. Ask players to move around the room, changing archetypes as they reach each 'station'.
- Add in a line from Shakespeare and ask your cast to move to each station and explore how a line sounds in the energy of that archetype.
- Experiment with unexpected archetypes. A Witch from *Macbeth* as the Carer, Hamlet as the Innocent.

Players	Age	Time
5+	8+	60

Characterisation, Energy, Improvisation, Physicality

Wants and Fears

A game to explore character motivation.

How to Play

Desire and fear are key motivators. Explain that characters will often do or say things either because they want something or they fear something.

Put out two chairs. Tell your cast that the first chair will represent what the character wants; the second chair will represent what the character fears.

When someone sits in the 'wants' chair they articulate something which that character wants, e.g. if you were working with Malvolio they might say, 'I want Olivia to love me.' In the 'fears' chair they articulate something the character is afraid of, e.g. 'I'm afraid everyone laughs at me behind my back.'

Ask the group to make sure there is always someone sitting in one of the chairs, i.e. as soon as a chair is vacated by one actor, another must fill it. This will increase the pace and encourage them to use their instincts to explore as many ideas as possible.

Depending on the ability of your cast, you may want to build in discussion about a specific character or group of characters in small groups, before asking for individual contributions.

The Aim of the Game

This game builds an understanding of key characters collaboratively, taking pressure off the leads and involving the ensemble. It helps actors untangle their character's web of motivation in a fun, physical way.

Variations and Extensions

Choose one or more key turning points in the play and play this game for the character at each of those points. This will help the actor see how their character develops over the course of the play.

Players	Age	Time
2+	10+	20

Analysis, Characterisation, Improvisation, Teamwork

Leading with Body Parts

An entertaining way to create character through movement.

How to Play

Tell the cast to move through the space and to allow their movement to be led by a certain body part, e.g. chest, nose, stomach, pelvis, toes or knees.

Encourage them to exaggerate this. Introduce a scale to help them regulate the level of performance – the most exaggerated movements are a level 10, the most subtle are a level 1. You will find the same body part at different levels produces very different characters – Caliban might be led by his nose at a level 10, Malvolio at a level 5, Helena at a level 1. Ask them to find a level they feel is suited to the character they are building.

Once the participants have had some time playing their physicality, you could begin to develop voices for these characters. Ask them to greet each other. What voice would a nose-led person have? What voice would a stomach-led person have? How would different characters relate and react to each other?

Ask some of the group to come out of character and to watch other people. Reflect on what characters and stories are emerging. Identify characters that remind you of someone in your play. You could introduce a few of that character's lines and see how they work with the physicality they have discovered.

The Aim of the Game

Shakespeare's plays are full of bold, sometimes supernatural, characters that need to be clearly differentiated on stage. This exercise will help your cast develop bold physical characters, progressing beyond more 'obvious' choices and presenting Shakespeare's characters in a unique and playful way.

Players	Age	Time
4+	6+	10
Characterisation, Focus, Physicality		

Role on the Wall

Simple, visual exercises to help actors create complex characters.

How to Play

We will use Lady Macbeth as an example here, but you can do this with most characters.

Draw the outline of a large gingerbread person on a piece of flipchart paper. With your cast, fill the inside of the outline with words that demonstrate how Lady Macbeth feels on the inside, e.g. ambitious, murderous, anxious, excited. Once you have built up a good number of words, on the outside of the figure write words that demonstrate how she wants the world to see her, e.g. composed, regal, feminine, kind.

Encourage your cast to think of evidence from the text for the words they choose, both for internal and external thoughts, e.g. what makes them think Lady Macbeth is ambitious?

When you are done, you will have created a more subtle, layered and in-depth understanding of the character for your whole company. You could ask them to do the same exercise for their own characters and stick these pictures to the walls of your rehearsal room to remind your actors of the complexity of their roles as they proceed through rehearsals.

The Aim of the Game

Shakespeare's characters are multifaceted, often saying one thing but meaning another – Lady Macbeth appears to be a consummate hostess but she is actually planning the murder of her guest of honour. This game will help your cast understand the nuances of their characters and to physicalise these for the audience. It is a good opportunity to start conversations about motivation and to build up a rounded understanding of characters based on the text.

Variations and Extensions

Sculpting

This extension allows participants to physicalise their discoveries about the interior and exterior of their characters.

As a group, choose one of the words from the inside of the character and one from the outside. Ask participants to get into pairs and label themselves A and B. A is the sculptor and B is the clay. Instruct A to move B gently into a freeze-frame position – they could issue verbal instructions or use mirroring if preferred. A should 'sculpt' B into two positions, one to represent the 'inside' characteristic and one to represent the 'outside' characteristic.

Once they have these two positions, ask B to move from one image into the other. What does the transition from outside to inside look like? What are the differences between the two? Can they find a physicality that suggests both?

You could add in language and ask B to speak from the different positions – how does the same line sound when spoken by 'gracious hostess' Lady Macbeth when compared to 'ruthlessly ambitious' Lady Macbeth? Once you have done this, swap over, so B now sculpts A.

You can extend this exercise by creating a scale across the room from 'inside' to 'outside'. Ask actors to move along this line, transforming as they go. You may discover interesting moments in the middle that work well for different scenes. Discuss these choices with your cast, e.g. where is Lady Macbeth on that scale when she welcomes King Duncan to the castle, compared to when she tries to calm Macbeth immediately after the murder?

Players	Age	Time
2+	10+	30

Analysis, Characterisation, Improvisation, Physicality, Teamwork

Floor Surfaces

A movement game to create character using an imagined environment.

How to Play

Ask the group to move through the room and balance the space. This means that they should spread themselves equally and, if they see empty space, they should move into it. Then ask the group to imagine that they are:

- Moving with very heavy shoes, or through a field of thick mud.
- Moving over ice.
- Moving over hot coals.
- Moving as if they are surrounded by light, fluffy clouds.

At different points, pause half the cast and ask them to watch the other half. Talk about what characters and stories they can see. Play with a 1-to-10 scale and see how that affects the physicalities created.

Now, identify a location from your play, e.g. a corpse-ridden battlefield, a large and luxurious palace, a dappled and fragrant forest clearing. Remember there are no right or wrong answers so try out whatever comes into your mind. We will take the battlefield as an example.

Ask your cast to move around the room with this in mind. How would they step on a battlefield filled with rotting dead bodies? Ask them to make their movements as big as possible, 10 out of 10.

Now remove the scenario of the battlefield and tell players to continue moving around the room in this way. They have created a character who moves in a very distinct, exaggerated way. Add in a line from your play and ask participants to say that line in the voice of the character they have just created.

Gradually scale the movement and voice back from a level 10 until you are at a level 1. At level 1 the movements are no longer exaggerated but they have created a character who still moves and speaks in a distinctive way.

Encouraging your actors to be creative with the stimulus gives them a way to physicalise their character that they might not have thought of. This work should be fun and you should encourage the company to embrace the grotesque. It is often a great way of creating comedic characters or over-the-top moments.

The Aim of the Game

Shakespeare's characters are often extraordinary people and creatures – monarchs, fairies, witches or warriors. Your players may find it challenging to adapt their physicality to present these characters. This game will help actors shrug off their own physicality and embrace alternative ways of moving and occupying space. It should help them to inhabit the world of the play as well as the bodies of their characters.

Players	Age	Time
2+	6+	15
Characterisation, Physicality		

48

CHARACTER

Shakespeare Zoo

A playful game for developing characters from the outside in.

How to Play

Tell everyone to choose an animal, or you may like to pick out of a hat. Ask them to think about that animal's movement and words to describe it.

You might like to give them choices: Is it fast or slow? Heavy or light? Are movements in certain body parts particularly pronounced? Does it take up a lot of space? What is the shape of its body?

Ask them to move around the space adopting that animal's qualities of movement. Be very clear that they are still a human, so they can walk on two legs, sit down, talk, etc., but they are embodying the qualities of the animal.

Encourage them to commit fully to this physicality and make bold choices. Call out different body parts and ask them just to locate the movement there. Once they've fully explored and committed, play with different levels on a 1-to-10 scale.

Next, explore what might happen when some of these animals meet each other. How do their reactions differ for different meetings?

Now ask players to layer emotions and human qualities on top of the animal character. Encourage them to think of emotions that might not be obvious to the animal they are portraying – e.g. a cowardly lion or a brave mouse, a snooty bear, or a bossy giraffe – and move around the space with this physicality. Ask half of the cast to stop moving and observe the others in action – are any of your Shakespeare characters emerging?

Once you have begun to identify certain characters you might want to introduce language – use *Ghosting* (game 35) so the actor doesn't have to hold a script and the physicality is maintained.

The Aim of the Game

Animals are a great way to think about the physicality of character, especially for young actors. It is also a technique used by many theatre professionals; for example, Antony Sher played Richard III inspired by the description of the character as 'a bottled spider'. This is a good game to play both before casting, to help you see which characters may suit each actor, or after, to help actors create a unique physicality. It also helps liberate actors from the script and preconceptions about 'Shakespearean' characters and acting.

Players	Age	Time
2+	6+	15
Characterisation, Physicality, Storytelling		

Shakespeare Status Games

A series of status games to help students portray character and relationships.

Many scenes in Shakespeare's plays are based on power struggles – characters trying to gain the upper hand in order to achieve an objective. Asking your actors to consider and play with the status of their character can change the whole dynamic of a scene. These games use status to develop character and help actors to explore a variety of tactics to alter their status on stage.

All Hail

One member of the group sits on a chair – that person is the king or queen. One by one, all the others must walk past and do something to impress the person sitting in the chair. Make sure that they're being as imaginative and varied as possible.

Discuss what worked and what was interesting to watch. Who is the king/queen in your play or scene? What changes if participants play this game in character?

Status Spectrum

Choose a scene with two characters sparring for status, e.g. Beatrice and Benedick. Set out two lines of ten chairs facing each other. One end of each line represents high status, the other end represents low status. Tell your actors 1 is the lowest status they could possibly be and 10 the highest.

Ask two actors to read the dialogue. They can move up and down along the line of chairs, as often as they want, as they feel their status is changing. They can move whether they are speaking or listening. Are the other character's words having an impact on their own status? Make sure your actors move gradually, one chair at a time – no jumps.

Watch this with the rest of your cast and reflect. Do you agree with where the characters ended up in their status line? Was there a moment that changed things for a character? How could you show the audience that moment if you take the chairs away?

This is a great game to use to help actors understand the spectrum of status. You could also use it for emotions, such as love or fear.

High Five

Again, choose a scene with two characters sparring for status, e.g. Oberon and Titania. Ask your actors to play the scene – they may read or you might find it useful to use *Ghosting* (game 35) to free them up to express their status level with their bodies as well as their voices. Ask two other players to position themselves behind the actors, one behind each. They must observe the scene and indicate the status of the actor opposite them by raising/lowering their hand. Level with their head indicates the highest possible status, on the floor indicates the lowest. They should be indicating the status of the opposing character, not the person that they are behind. You want the actors to see their own status and respond accordingly.

Reflect with your cast. What tactics did each character use to improve their status? What was most effective? What was it like as an actor to see their status physicalised in this way? Were there any surprises?

The Aim of the Games

These games are all playful ways to demonstrate the importance of status to characterisation and to see the impact that changing status can have on a scene.

+ chairs		
Players	Age	Time
2+	10+	15
Analysis, Characterisation, Energy		

The Court Makes the King

A collaborative game to demonstrates the importance of the ensemble in storytelling.

How to Play

Choose an area of your rehearsal space to be 'the stage' and bring one of your central characters into this space. This should be a high-status character, such as Macbeth or Olivia. This will be your 'King'.

Ask roughly half of your cast to form an active audience. They will be observing the action and making assumptions about the characters on stage based on what they see. The other half of the group will join the 'King' on stage – this is the ensemble.

Tell the 'King' that they aren't going to do any acting. They should simply move around the stage space as they normally would, occasionally stopping and taking in their surroundings if they feel like it.

Give the ensemble simple instructions that react to the movements of the King, e.g. they must always remain behind the King; if the King looks at them, they must look at the ground; they must always be smaller than the King…

Be playful with your suggestions and adapt them to the character, e.g. if Claudius is on stage, you could tell your ensemble to avoid eye contact to demonstrate their fear and suspicion of him.

After a few minutes of action, ask your audience to feed back – what kind of monarch/leader/person of high status is this? What did they see on stage to make them think that?

A fun variation on this game is to give the ensemble a secret objective (which the audience and King don't hear), e.g. the King has toilet roll stuck to their shoe and doesn't know. Watch this and ask the audience how this character has changed.

The Aim of the Game

This game is particularly helpful where young actors believe they are only performing if they are speaking, or that the named characters are much more significant. This game demonstrates the importance of the ensemble and their reactions. It is a great way to support the principal characters as it takes some of the pressure off them on stage. It will also help your cast develop a directorial eye as they observe what is effective on stage.

Players	Age	Time
10+	8+	15
Characterisation, Imagination, Improvisation, Teamwork		

Reaction Box

A game to develop strong ensemble reactions.

How to Play

Ask everyone to get into a position where they can see you. Ask players to look at you and imagine that you are holding a box. Inside the box is something extraordinary. Tell them that when you open this box you are going to ask for a reaction, and you want to see that reaction in every part of their bodies and faces. Ask them to focus on the box and anticipate what will be in it.

When they are all focused and ready, eager to see what is in the box, tell them the reaction that you expect – e.g. 'joy!' – and then mime opening the box. You could also try:

- Fear.
- Disgust.
- Anger.
- Confusion.
- Horror.
- Satisfaction.

What is in the box doesn't matter. Encourage your cast to embody and exaggerate their reactions fully so the audience is in no doubt as to what they are feeling.

Play with different combinations of reactions. For instance, ask them to be fearful of what is inside the box before it is opened. Then, when the revelation comes, its contents actually bring huge relief. You could also try telling them that the contents of the box inspire one emotion, but they should conceal it with another, e.g. the box's contents make them angry, but they must try and pretend to be joyful. What does that look and feel like?

Play with half of the cast while the rest of them watch. Ask a player to open the box so that you can watch too. Discuss which scenes these reactions could apply to. Try running the scenes immediately afterwards and asking your actors to apply the reactions that they just played with. Reflect on the importance of reactions – the reactions of the ensemble are just as important as the words of the lead actors in communicating the story to the audience.

The Aim of the Game

Shakespeare's plays are full of revelations, sudden dramatic events and messengers bringing good or bad news, e.g. Bottom entering as a donkey in *A Midsummer Night's Dream*; news of Hermione's death in *The Winter's Tale*. The stories demand that these moments resonate with everyone on stage, including ensemble or background actors. Often actors forget the size of reaction required – they need to hear these things happening as if for the first time. This game is a fun way to work on ensemble reactions and demonstrate their importance to your actors.

Players	Age	Time
4+	6+	20
Characterisation, Focus, Physicality, Teamwork		

Oh Yes!

A fun way to create ensemble reactions and bring energy to dialogue.

How to Play

Choose a scene to work with in which there are several non-speaking or background characters. Ask your actors to run the scene with the following instruction (this is for everyone, including the ensemble):

- When they hear a piece of information that is new for their character, they should clap their hands once.

Reflect on the moments that were highlighted. What does it reveal about individual characters' stories? Where did characters know or not know different things?

Now, run the scene again but layer in the following reactions:

- Something their character disagrees with or reacts negatively towards: 'No way!'
- Something their character supports or reacts positively towards: 'Oh yes!'

The reaction phrases are suggestions, work with the group on their own versions. What would they say? Or what would the characters in this world say?

Finally, run the scene again, but ask actors to internalise their reactions. How are they going to tell the audience how their character is feeling and responding? What tools do they have at their disposal?, e.g. facial expressions, focus, spatial relationships, etc.

Remind actors that they have worked really hard to know the story but the audience don't know what they do. Their reactions on stage will tell the audience what is shocking, funny, upsetting and so on.

The Aim of the Game

Often in Shakespeare's plays a lot of information is delivered quickly, and characters need to react differently from each other. In the final scene of *Twelfth Night*, Viola reveals herself as a woman when most people thought she was a man, Sebastian arrives when Viola thought he was dead, Viola and Orsino discover they love each other, and Sebastian and Olivia reveal they have secretly married. It can be hard to untangle who knows what and how different characters would react. This game is useful for engaging everyone on stage with the central events, clarifying differences in reaction, and bringing energy to scenes that are heavy in dialogue and exposition.

+ a scene from your play		
Players	Age	Time
2+	10+	15
Characterisation, Energy, Storytelling		

Strings

An inclusive game to clarify character relationships.

How to Play

Ask your cast to get into pairs, facing each other. Each pair should imagine that they have an invisible string connecting them. Every time they move, they must keep the same distance between each other. Invite them to try moving around the space, maintaining their invisible string, and not letting it sag or break. They don't need to continue to face each other but they must not let the string get longer or shorter.

Ask players to feed back on what that was like to do. What needs to happen in order to make it successful? Try playing with a very large distance between pairs, and then with a very small distance. Reflect on the difference. It might be helpful for some of the cast to watch some pairs move around and discuss what stories they seem to be telling using this invisible string.

Now ask the pairs to label themselves A and B. Explain that you are going to give them characters, and each must make an individual choice about how long they want the string to be between them and the other person. Note that the length of string that A wants may not be the same as the length B wants.

Give scenarios from your play, e.g.:

A: Duke.
B: Servant secretly in love with the Duke.

A: Fairy waiting on the Queen.
B: Fairy Queen.

A: Soldier.
B: Soldier's enemy.

At this stage they can let their character inform how they move too, e.g. a soldier might march.

Watch some of these scenes back and reflect on how much of the story has been shared through the distance that each character chooses or attempts to place between themselves and another. What happens when one character wants to be very near someone who, by contrast, wants to be very far away from them? How could you use these moments in your play?

The Aim of the Game

This is a simple game to get actors thinking about character relationships and status dynamics, portraying them on stage in a simple, visual way.

Players	Age	Time
6+	10+	10
Characterisation, Imagination, Storytelling, Teamwork		

Character Profiles

A game to develop individual characters in ensemble scenes.

How to Play

Choose a scene with a lot of ensemble characters on stage, e.g. the shipwreck scene in *The Tempest*. Ask each member of the ensemble to find their own space and close their eyes (the named characters in the scene can also take part). Explain that within the ensemble each actor is a distinct character living in the world of the play. You are going to guide everyone through a series of questions. It will be a series of quick choices and there are no wrong answers. They must answer in character, in their heads:

- What is your name?
- How old are you?
- What are you wearing?
- Where do you live? What is your favourite food? What makes you most happy? What are you most scared of? What really annoys you?
- *Ask a question that relates to the context of the scene*: Are you a passenger or do you work on board the ship? Passengers – why are you on the voyage? Workers – what is your job?
- *Ask a question about another character in the scene*: How do you feel about Alonso? Is he a good king? Does he treat you well?
- *Ask a question about an event in the scene*: Have you weathered a lot of storms? Do you get scared, or seasick? Do you think someone should have done something earlier to avoid it?
- *Ask a question about something that is said in the scene*: How you feel when Gonzalo says 'The king and prince at prayers/Let's assist them, for our case is as theirs'?

You can make the questions as detailed as you like. It will take a bit of preparation time to identify the questions that are central to the scene, but it's worth it to shape the choices of your actors effectively.

Now tell actors that when you say 'Go', it will be twenty seconds before the start of the scene. They should think of one thing that their character is going to do in those twenty seconds. It should be something possible in this space (whatever your stage represents in that moment, in this case the deck of a ship). Say 'Go.' Run the twenty seconds and then start the scene.

Ask players what it felt like. What kind of characters could they see? What was the atmosphere like? Did they see reactions?

The Aim of the Game

Many of Shakespeare's scenes have scope for unnamed background characters, such as those set at parties, markets, on board ships, etc. Despite having few or no lines, these characters are vital for setting the scene and telling the audience how to react. This game will inspire choices for many actors at once. It should enliven ensemble scenes and give actors a better understanding and ownership of the world of the play.

Players	Age	Time
2+	10+	15

Analysis, Characterisation, Focus, Imagination

PART SIX

STAGING

'Think when we talk of horses,
that you see them'
Henry V

Shakespeare's plays are peppered with battles and shipwrecks, love scenes and murder, forests and castles. Writing in an era before stage lighting and special effects, he did not let himself be limited by the resources available to his actors – he trusted them to create stage pictures worthy of his words.

In this section we help you to do the same, using your actors' voices, bodies and creativity to put the story on the stage. We focus on moments that might be challenging to stage – big movement sequences, fights, battles and intimate love scenes. These games will empower the ensemble, making sure that every actor is contributing to the story and the show, even if they are playing a background character.

The Game of Power

A game to illustrate the importance of stage composition.

How to Play

Tell your cast that they will be an audience of directors and agree on a stage space. Start by asking one actor to position themselves on stage in the position they feel is most powerful. Then invite another actor to enter the space and take up a more powerful position – they should be aiming to take the power away from the first actor. The first actor is not allowed to change their position. Discuss with the audience whether this attempt to seize power was effective and why.

Repeat this until four or five actors are in the space. Ask the audience to comment on who was successful in becoming the most powerful person on stage. Be sure to point out any surprises. What stories and characters are emerging from these bodies on stage? Can they see any characters from their own play, e.g. Could that be Iago lurking in the corner? Could Juliet be the actor centre-stage, who had all her power removed by the others? What scene from the play does this look like?

You can start to explore which areas of the stage imply power and status, and discuss which characters from your play should move towards these areas. The idea of power in the space can be a useful reference point for you when you are working on specific scenes later.

The Aim of the Game

Many of Shakespeare's plays are about power struggles – fathers against daughters, soldiers against kings, fairy queens against fairy kings. This game quickly illuminates composition and how bodies positioned in space can tell a clear story of power and status. It will also help you build a shared language with your cast that you can return to throughout rehearsals.

Variations and Extensions

You can also use this exercise to explore how and where audiences focus their attention. In this version, each actor is trying to draw focus to themselves. Although actors must still commit to one position on stage, they can attempt to recapture the focus after the entry of another actor by altering their body, level or eyeline, e.g. an actor might choose to crouch down if everyone else is standing up, or look up when everyone else is looking out to the audience.

Players	Age	Time
6+	10+	20

Analysis, Characterisation, Focus, Physicality

Attract/Repel

A simple way to frame movement choices to depict characters' relationships.

How to Play

Choose a scene. This game works well with duologues about persuasion, e.g. Richard III attempting to woo Lady Anne, Calpurnia trying to convince Caesar to stay at home, Lady Macbeth persuading Macbeth to kill Duncan. Tell your actors that they are going to make a definite movement every time their character speaks. They have three options:

1. *Attract*: Move toward another person.
2. *Repel*: Move away from another person.
3. *Remain still* (this must be an active choice).

Ask two other players to position themselves at the back of the stage as 'ghosts' and deliver the characters' lines (see *Ghosting*, game 35, for a full version of this game). Everyone else should be watching the scene as an active audience. Having the lines spoken for them means the actors can listen and focus purely on their movement choices. Reflect with your cast on which moments in the text caused an attract/repel and why.

Now ask the ghosts to feed the actors their lines. The ghosts should speak neutrally and the actors should repeat the words with intention. The actors should continue to move according to the attract/repel choices. Reflect with your actors on how this felt. Ask the audience how the movement helped to tell the story for them? Why did actors choose to move at different points? Where did they change their direction of movement?

The Aim of the Game

Shakespeare's scripts are predominantly dialogue, with very few stage directions, so it's easy for scenes to become stationary when actors aren't confident inventing movement. This can make the scenes seem flat, when in fact the energy and power dynamics should be constantly fluctuating as characters manoeuvre to gain the upper hand. This game physicalises these shifts, helping actors develop understanding of their characters and bringing life to static scenes.

Variations and Extensions

This can also work with objects, e.g. Macbeth's 'Is this a dagger?' soliloquy. The actor should be attracted or repelled by the object as they work through the decision with themselves. You can use a real or imagined object or spot in the room (see *Chair Swap*, game 29, for a variation that works well with soliloquies.

You can also use this for persuasive speeches, e.g. Mark Antony's speech in *Julius Caesar*. In this case, the crowd should be attracted or repelled by the words of the character.

+ a scene from your play		
Players	**Age**	**Time**
4+	10+	20
Analysis, Characterisation, Physicality, Storytelling		

Stop-Go

A useful call-and-response game for ensemble moments and transitions.

How to Play

Start with two simple instructions:

- *Go*: Actors move around the space, filling all the gaps and balancing the space.
- *Stop*: An active stop, as though you've pressed pause.

Continue with these two instructions until players are confident with them. From here you can layer in any commands you want. You may start to incorporate words or ideas from your play – we will use *A Midsummer Night's Dream* as an example below.

- *Clear the space*: Actors move into the wings, or to the side of the space, keeping the energy and focus directed towards the performance area.
- *Slow motion*: Actors continue following the previous instruction, slowed down.
- *Swipe*: Actors who have cleared the space swap sides and specific actors are left on stage, e.g. the lovers are left on stage (this is very useful for transitions).
- *Centre*: Form a tight bunch centre-stage.
- *Sky*: Look up. It can be useful for the actors to do this over a count of three.
- *Audience*: Look out to the audience. Can be a quick movement or over a specific count.
- *Reach*: Make a reaching gesture to someone across the space (this can also be very effective out to the audience).
- *Wither*: Over a count of ten seconds, do whatever 'wither' means to you. Later, give the actors something specific to wither into, e.g. 'Wither into sleeping fairies.'
- *Grow*: Over a count, do whatever 'grow' means to you. Later give them something specific to grow in to, e.g. 'Grow into trees in the forest.'

- *Survivor*: One or two people are left standing while everyone else withers. You can specify who survives or let the ensemble choose.
- *Sacrifice*: One or two people wither while everyone else remains.

Ask some of your cast to watch as the others play, so they can see how effective this work is for an audience and help you identify interesting moments to use in your final production.

The Aim of the Game

This game is a good way to get actors used to following simple commands quickly. This is useful for choreographing big, fluid movement sequences that fill the stage, as well as for creating transitions. It should also encourage actors to think like directors and apply stagecraft to the story of the play.

Variations and Extensions

Once your cast are accustomed to the directions you can start to flavour them for specific locations or scenes. Taking a battlefield as an example, 'Go' could mean moving as exhausted soldiers through a muddy field. 'Centre', huddling around a fire. 'Reach', an attack on someone else. 'Grow' into a heated battle and 'Wither' into dead bodies.

You could organise the different commands into a sequence which is the same every time and which your cast can learn. You may have a cast member giving the commands, or you may use music to cue them. An alternative is to take the commands out entirely, and let the company make decisions together (without speaking) in the moment as a way to build teamwork and focus.

We recommend that you play music in order to create a more immersive experience for players.

Players	Age	Time
5+	6+	10
Focus, Memory, Physicality, Teamwork		

Three Gestures

A game to stage group scenes quickly.

How to Play

Choose a scene with lots of people on stage. We'll take a banquet as an example. Ask your cast what this banquet is like, and what people might do there. Ask them to think specifically about their character and what they would be doing (you might like to run *Character Profiles*, game 54, before this).

Inspired by this feedback, ask everyone to create three gestures. Encourage them to try lots of things out and choose their favourites. Each actor will have their own three gestures and should number them.

Count the group through their three gestures, i.e. when you say 'one' everyone performs their first gesture and so on. You will probably want to encourage them to be bigger – ask them to turn the dial up to a level 10.

Take the time to play. Change the tempo and rhythm, add sounds, encourage changes in levels.

Rehearse a few more times so the actors are confident in their sequence and then arrange them in the space according to the scene, e.g. for a banquet they might be sitting as though around a table.

Play the moves again. Ask everyone to find at least one moment of interaction with someone else near them.

Add in a fourth gesture that the whole group do together, e.g. a big 'cheers' for a banquet.

Rehearse the sequence a few times on a loop.

To stage this in your show, you could time the gestures to music, or simple percussion.

The Aim of the Game

Shakespeare's plays are sprawling – often taking place in big spaces with many characters. This is very helpful when you are working with big groups, but also means you must create scenes with many people on stage and keep a lot of young actors focused at once. This exercise creates a rich, visually pleasing sequence in which each actor only needs to remember their own individual movements. It can be used for any group movement, e.g. sailors on a ship, a battle, a busy market, a party scene.

Variations and Extensions

Gestures lend themselves to more static scenes but could work layered onto movement, e.g. actors could identify four points on stage, one for the performance of each gesture, which they move between.

Players	Age	Time
6+	6+	15

Characterisation, Energy, Focus, Physicality, Rhythm, Teamwork

Mirroring

A physical way to express character relationships.

How to Play

Ask your company to pair up and label themselves A and B. Play some gentle music. A starts by moving one hand very slowly, so that B can copy. B should be as precise as possible, they want to mirror A exactly. A should take care of their partner, going at a speed that they can copy easily. The pairs should aim to make it impossible to tell who is leading and who is following.

Once they've got the hang of it they can extend the movement beyond their hand, ensuring that they are going slowly and not moving in a way that means their partner can't see them. Swap so that Bs have a chance to lead and As to copy.

In your show, this can be a really simple way to show a close relationship between two characters, be that love, friendship or a familial bond. It's a good way to introduce twins!

The Aim of the Game

Shakespeare's plays contain intense emotions that young people may not have experienced personally. This game is a useful way to portray character relationships and emotions, both love and hate, in an accessible manner. It's also a great way to relax and focus a company, and to build teamwork and observation skills.

Variations and Extensions

Love

Shakespeare wrote some of the world's most iconic love stories. Very occasionally, two people are in love with each other and talk about it openly or kiss, e.g. Romeo and Juliet, Beatrice and Benedick (eventually). However, often the attraction is only implied and must be manifested outside the text, and these choices can be very difficult for young actors who are just finding their feet in the world of love. This variation is useful for two characters that need to demonstrate love on stage without specifically speaking about it, e.g. Rosalind and Orlando in *As You Like It*.

Ask your actors to play the scene. (If they don't know their lines yet, use *Ghosting*, game 35, to feed the lines as this exercise is tricky with scripts in hands.) Give one actor the note to mirror everything the other person does, i.e. copy all their movements. Ask them to be precise and mirror even the tiniest movement. You might like to keep this as a secret note so the person they're mirroring doesn't feel or appear self-conscious.

Reflect with both actors on what that was like to do. How did it feel to have your attention focused so strongly on another person? How did it feel to have someone reflecting your body language? Reflect on any moments you like and would like to keep in your scene. It may be that you want to turn the dial up/down on the mirroring, or to pick out specific things for your actor to mirror. It is important to keep it live, so your actors are playing the game on stage rather than just memorising simultaneous movements.

This game works because people do mirror body language when they are attracted to someone. It's a more sophisticated, less obvious signifier of attraction than kissing and a lot more comfortable for young actors.

Conflict

Sometimes the intense relationship you want to portray is about conflict rather than love.

Actors should get into A/B pairs again. A holds their hand, palm-forward, about ten inches from B's face. The aim is for B's face to follow A's hand, always keeping that same distance. If A's hand tilts, B's face does too. Encourage A to take it slowly and be specific about their movement – it is most effective when the space between them stays constant.

Invite As to take their partner on a journey around the room and experiment with different levels. Remind them that they are responsible for their partner in the space and should take care of them –

this game doubles as a trust exercise. Now Bs can take over at any point by simply raising their hand to A's face. Let them try swapping a few times until they are able to be quick and fluid.

This game physicalises the battle for supremacy that characterises many of Shakespeare's scenes. You could use it to choreograph a fight by layering in the intention to hurt each other. You might want to model some moves, e.g. they might 'throw', 'push' or 'drag' each other, always keeping that same distance between palm and face. Remind them always to make it slow and to keep each other safe.

Conflict Extension

B's body mirrors the tension in A's hand. How is their body affected by a stiff hand? By a scrunched hand? By a relaxed waving hand?

One person can control two other people who follow one hand each.

One person could control a whole group. Each person chooses a specific part of the leader's body, and their whole body is led by the movement of that one part. This can produce some impressive movement sequences with one person holding ultimate power, e.g. Henry V or Macbeth in battle, or Oberon or Prospero ruling over others.

+ gentle music		
Players	**Age**	**Time**
2+	10+	30
Characterisation, Focus, Physicality, Teamwork		

Round, Across, Under

A game for staging fight scenes.

How to Play

Tell your cast that they are going to be creating some movements inspired by the words 'Round, Across, Under'. In pairs, each person invents three moves to practise on their partner. For now, they are simply neutral gestures, not blows or anything to do with combat. Encourage them to use different body parts to create their gestures, not just their hands, e.g. they might move their hand around their partner's head, then their elbow across their partner's torso, then their foot under their partner's leg. The rules of the movements are that they must be specific, have a definite start and end point, be in slow motion and with no actual contact made.

When both actors have come up with their moves, they should alternate them to make a sequence of six – round, round, across, across, under, under. Ask them to run this repeatedly in a cycle until the sequence is fluid. Ensure the pairs are running their sequence in super-slow motion. Keep emphasising this because they will speed up!

If they're not doing so already, ask them to react to their partner's gestures. So, every 'round', 'across' or 'under' should elicit a corresponding movement, e.g. moving their elbow across their partner's torso might make them lean back to avoid it.

Now encourage them to show an intention to hurt each other, e.g. through facial expressions. Remind them to continue moving in slow motion. Invite them to vocalise their gestures and reactions. Add appropriate music to underscore.

You should see interesting and convincing sequences that involve no physical contact. This could be two people in hand-to-hand combat, or lots of pairs around the stage in a street brawl or battle sequence.

The Aim of the Game

Shakespeare's plays contain many dramatic fights, often to the death. This exercise is a fun way to create believable (and safe) stage combat to fit any fight.

Variations and Extensions

Put in an onstage crowd watching and reacting to the action. If you have difficulty getting them to react convincingly, ask them to be specific by deciding whose side they're on, then choose just one gesture in the sequence to react to.

Put distance between the fighters, so they are still making and reacting to the same moves but are metres apart. This looks impressive and will give you peace of mind if they are very exuberant with their gestures.

Once they know the sequence well, turn them 90 degrees out so the audience can see their movements and facial expressions. This means they are now side by side with their partner, rather than facing them, but reacting to their partner's movements as though they are engaged in a fight. Make sure they stay in time with each other – music can help with this.

Chair Sequences

This variation works well if you have an actor who uses a wheelchair, or to create interesting levels with any players. It can also be used for creating visually interesting scenes that are not about conflict, e.g. Roman senators plotting to kill the emperor, or a ghost haunting their son.

Ask players to get into groups of four – one person should sit on a chair, two people stand on either side of them, and one person stands behind them. This can be adapted depending on your group, so that more people are sitting or standing instead.

Ask the group to create movements for the following words. Everyone should be part of what's happening:

- *Over*: Two people could shake hands, with another person looking up from underneath.

- *Around*: Someone could move around another member of the team.
- *Beside*: Two people could stand back to back, so that they are next to each other.
- *Level change*: A person sitting on the chair could stand on it, or someone standing could move down to one knee.

Once they have created the movements, you can add music. These sequences are a great way to show the relationships between characters – the character with the chair can be the most powerful, or the least. A simple change of level can tell a huge story – a group of characters who suddenly kneel before someone can show that this person has become very powerful. This is a way to tell stories without using words and use your actors' creativity to choreograph movement sequences.

+ atmospheric music, a chair (optional)		
Players	**Age**	**Time**
2+	10+	15
Focus, Memory, Physicality, Storytelling, Teamwork		

Join the Dots

A playful, physical way to stage ensemble scenes.

How to Play

Ask everyone to pick three very specific parts of their body, e.g. tip of the left index finger or their right knee cap. They should number each body part 1, 2 and 3 and then point to each in that order. Warn them that they should pick a part of their body that they would be comfortable with someone else touching. Encourage them to choose body parts at different levels, e.g. one high up like their forehead and one low down like their left ankle.

Ask the group to get into pairs. As you call out, '1, 2, 3', partners have to find a way to connect the corresponding body parts, e.g. number 1, the tip of the left index finger of partner A should connect to number 1, the right kneecap of partner B. Once they are used to the rhythm, you can stop calling out the numbers and ask the pairs to continue at their own pace, creating a sequence with the three connections.

Next, tell the group that they don't have to stay in one place and can move through the space. Add in some atmospheric music. Ask one half of the group at a time to watch the other and comment on what they see. Ask them if they can see any stories or characters developing.

Finally, give the group a title or a theme, e.g. a battle or friendship. See how the quality of movement is influenced. Encourage them to use facial expressions and changing pace to demonstrate their theme. You will find that you have quickly choreographed rich, interesting scenes without having to plan minutely or be too prescriptive in your instructions.

The Aim of the Game

Some young actors will find it difficult to express themselves physically on stage, particularly when it comes to unfamiliar scenarios or intimate scenes.

This exercise will free them up to be creative with their physicality by giving them specific, manageable instructions. It can be used to choreograph big ensemble moments, such as fight scenes or shipwrecks, or more intimate moments between characters.

Variations and Extensions

Coloured Dots

It may be easier for your students to have a constant visual cue, rather than having to remember the three spots they and they partner have chosen. Divide the group into pairs and stick three coloured dots (stickers) on the different parts of each person's body, or invite them do so themselves. Instead of calling out '1, 2, 3' as instructions, say 'red, yellow, green'. Each pair must then connect the dots (one at a time) to the corresponding coloured dot on their partner. They should then practise doing this in a sequence.

Add Distance

Try moving the pair further apart and repeat the sequence at different distances. This can help create intimate moments between characters without your cast members having to touch, e.g. Romeo reaching his hand toward Juliet's shoulder across the space.

+ atmospheric music, coloured stickers (optional)

Players	Age	Time
2+	8+	20

Improvisation, Physicality, Rhythm, Teamwork

Flock of Birds

A simple, collaborative way to stage impressive-looking movement sequences.

How to Play

Tell the cast to get into groups of four and arrange themselves in a diamond shape, all facing in the same direction so that one person can be seen by all the other members of the group. This person is the leader.

The leader should move their arms and bodies very slowly, as if moving on the Moon or under water. (You will have to keep reminding them of this.) The movements they make must be big and visible to the rest of their group, i.e. to the sides of their body, not in front. The rest of each group should copy everything their leader does. The slower the leader goes, the more accurately the rest of their group will be able to follow them.

When the leader would like to pass the leadership on, they should allow their movement to turn their bodies to the right or left, and a new person will automatically become the new leader because they are now the person at the front of the diamond shape that the rest of the group can see. Encourage them to make this transition of leaders as smooth as possible, without stopping the movement.

Once your cast have got the hang of this you can make their movement specific to your Shakespearean scene, e.g. imagine they are flying, rigging a ship, saying goodbye.

Add music to influence the 'mood' of the groups. You could also add in lines from your script, either spoken by someone from within the group, or by a different cast member.

Let participants watch each other so they can appreciate how effective this exercise is for the audience and understand the emotional impact of their work. This game is great for working with the whole cast and ensuring everyone is involved in creating stage pictures for their audience.

The Aim of the Game

Shakespeare's stories are full of epic scenes – balls and battles, weddings and shipwrecks. This exercise will help you to stage these big scenes quickly and stylishly, without having to direct each individual actor.

Variations and Extensions

Stagger the groups in amongst each other so they are muddled up but still following the same leader.

Ask two groups to face each other and enact a slow-motion battle/a goodbye/love at first sight/a dance (depending on which scenes you want to work with), responding to the movements of the opposing group. Play with the proximity of the groups – perhaps they could be very close together or very far apart.

+ music (optional)		
Players	Age	Time
8+	6+	20
Energy, Focus, Physicality, Storytelling, Teamwork		

Shakespeare's Footsteps

A fun twist on 'Grandmother's Footsteps' which helps build an ensemble and create a performance.

How to Play

Ask one player to position themselves at one end of the room with their back to the rest of the group. They are Shakespeare (or you can choose a character from your play). The rest of the group start at the other end of the room. Players try to get close enough to touch Shakespeare on the shoulder. Shakespeare can turn around at any point. If they see anyone moving then that person is sent back to the start line. You could add a line from your play to send them back, e.g. 'Fairies, skip hence.' Try adding some obstacles to reaching Shakespeare, e.g. everyone has to put on a hat.

After you have played it once, split the group in half and ask one group to reflect upon what they saw. Encourage them to talk about which bits were exciting or funny, and why. Did any characters stand out? Were they rooting for anyone in particular? Reflect on what it is like for an audience to watch a character try to achieve an objective, what it feels like when they succeed or are thwarted.

The Aim of the Game

This game will encourage teamwork and collaboration, and should inspire players to think about effective stagecraft. You can also use this game to stage moments in your production (see extensions below), as it contains all the elements of intrigue and tension that audiences love.

Variations and Extensions

You could give the group a character or intention from your play. For this version, the person at the front of the room is free to move around the space, and the rest of the group need to follow them, e.g.:

- *Soldiers* – The group are tired soldiers returning from battle. They have to move in a straight line, all together. Whenever the person at the front turns around, they can shout 'Attention!' to check that the group are all still and paying attention.

- *Courtiers* – The person at the front is the king or queen. When they turn to look at the group, everyone must bow. However, when their back is turned, the followers can try to play tricks on the king or queen.

Invisible Shakespeare

Take away the person playing Shakespeare and ask the group to play the game by imagining that someone is still there and turning around periodically. The group will all need to freeze at the same time, and you will send anyone who freezes too late back to the start. This will test their ability to work together and use their imaginations as well as creating an interesting performance.

Guards of the Gate

This is variation that could be used to stage a scene with careless guards or watchmen, or characters making sneaky entrances and exits, e.g. Romeo entering the Capulets' garden.

Two of your cast will be the guards. They should stand or sit close together with their backs to the rest of the group and their hands by their sides. They should leave a small space between them, about the width of another person. The rest of the group position themselves behind these two guards. One by one, everyone must try to sneak through the gap between the two guards without the guards hearing, seeing or realising. If the guards think that they can feel or hear something, they can lift their arms to try to catch the culprit – but they cannot turn around. The guards aim is to catch as many people as possible. You could ask the guards to close their eyes to make the game even trickier.

+ objects/props (optional)		
Players	**Age**	**Time**
10+	6+	10
Focus, Teamwork		

Cat and Mouse

A fun ensemble game for staging pursuit scenes.

How to Play

Ask twelve players to position themselves in a 3 x 4 grid system, arm's length from each other. (If you have spots of the type used in PE classes, lay them out and ask players to simply stand on them, or mark the floor with chalk.) You can change the size of the grid depending on the size of your cast, e.g. 3 x 3 or 4 x 4.

Tell everyone to face the same way and hold out their arms horizontally to form corridors. Tell actors that when you clap, everyone should turn 90 degrees to their right, therefore shifting the formation of the corridors. The next clap means they should turn back to their original position.

Now add a player to be the cat and one to be the mouse. The cat is trying to catch the mouse, the mouse is trying to stay away from the cat. They should enter at different parts of the grid, then the cat chases the mouse up and down the human corridors, which keep shifting at each clap. Play a few times until everyone gets the hang of it. Notice which bits are interesting dramatically – usually when the shifting corridors suddenly brought the cat and mouse close together, or thwarted the cat's plan.

It is time to layer in the circumstances of your play. Make sure everyone has a role to play, e.g. if you were directing *A Midsummer Night's Dream*, the ensemble could become trees in a forest, the cat would be Helena and the mouse Demetrius. If you were directing *Romeo and Juliet*, the ensemble could be revellers at the Capulet ball, the cat Romeo and the mouse Juliet. You could layer in the language of the script as they play. Encourage the ensemble to have opinions and attitudes to the scene rather than being passive – do they want Romeo to find Juliet? Are they keen to help Helena or Demetrius?

The Aim of the Game

Shakespeare made good use of the entertainment inherent in pursuit. His plays are full of characters chasing one another through forests, around islands and across dance floors. This is a quick and easy way to create chase scenes with real stakes. Because the movement of the ensemble determines the success or failure of the characters in real time, it's both fun for them, and engaging for the audience.

Variations and Extensions

You could play this game with actors working on soliloquies, particularly those that demonstrate indecision or a troubled mind, e.g. Hamlet, Lady Macbeth or King Lear. The actor would say their speech as they paced the corridors, and you could time shifts in thought, tone or pace with your claps. For some soliloquies the mouse they are pursuing could be an idea/desire that they want to catch.

+ floor spots/chalk (optional)		
Players	Age	Time
10+	8+	15
Characterisation, Physicality, Teamwork		

Sound Orchestra

An ensemble game to create a soundscape for your play.

How to Play

Choose an environment from your play, e.g. the forest from *As You Like It*. Start by asking the group to create sounds that they would hear in the forest. You could ask players to work individually or in pairs and small groups. Ask each pair or person to choose one forest sound and add an action to it. Sounds can be vocal, but could also use body percussion, e.g. tapping fingers on the floor as rain.

Once the group have invented their sounds, make a semicircle with everyone in it. Choose someone to position themselves in front of the semicircle, facing the group. This person is the 'Orchestra Conductor', who can use the following actions:

- *Gesture towards one pair or group*: The pair or group make their sound.
- *Close your hand*: The pair stop making their sound.
- *Gesture towards whole group*: The whole group make their sound.
- *Hands up high*: The sound gets louder.
- *Hands down low*: The sound gets quieter.
- *Point to one sound and then to the whole group*: Everyone does the same sound as that person.

Your company will create a 'soundscape' that you can use to set the scene or help transition between environments on stage.

The Aim of the Game

The company will create interesting aural environments for your production and gain a deeper ownership of the play. This also makes a good vocal warm-up before a performance.

Players	Age	Time
10+	6+	20

Focus, Imagination, Teamwork, Voice

Hot Spots

A game to create atmospheres and environments.

How to Play

Ask the cast to spread around the space and, individually or in pairs, create a sound and action for the environment of your play. The action and sound don't have to match, e.g. a bird sound doesn't need an action of flapping wings. When everyone has created and practised their sound and action, ask them to pick their 'hot spot'. This is a point in the room that will trigger their sound and action if someone moves past it. It should be a clear spot that they can see, and not directly in front of them.

One person is then nominated to go on a journey around the environment. Tell the others that, whenever the person moves past their hot spot, they should come to life with their sound and action. This should bring depth, variety and interest to the environment. Note any reactions the person moving round the room has to the sounds and actions.

You can then get characters from your play to travel around, e.g. Rosaline and Celia, who have just entered the forest. Encourage them to react to the sounds. Are they scared? Intrigued? The characters in your play now exist in a specific environment that informs the scene and the story.

You could bring this work in to your final production – perhaps at the start of a scene to transform the stage space into somewhere new.

The Aim of the Game

This exercise will help your cast to immerse themselves in the weird and wonderful worlds that Shakespeare created, making believable environments for their audience.

Players	Age	Time
10+	6+	15
Energy, Imagination, Teamwork		

APPENDICES

Ten-point Summary: *Macbeth*

The example ten-point summary and character cards which follow are both for *Macbeth*, and can be used with *Ten Events* (game 14) and *Character Cards* (game 17).

These are the ten events for *Macbeth* used by Coram Shakespeare Schools Foundation.

1. We are in Scotland, in the realm of King Duncan where two royal thanes – Macbeth and Banquo – are returning from war. They meet three witches who predict that Macbeth will become king, and that the children of Banquo will be kings.
2. Macbeth reports the news to his wife, Lady Macbeth, who tells him he must kill King Duncan. King Duncan arrives at the Castle as Macbeth and Lady Macbeth argue over whether to kill him or not.
3. Macbeth kills Duncan as he sleeps.
4. Duncan's son Malcolm is initially blamed for his father's killing and flees in fear, leaving Macbeth to be crowned king.
5. Macbeth has Banquo killed but Banquo's son escapes. Macbeth is haunted by his friend's ghost at a banquet.
6. Macbeth returns to the witches. They tell him to beware Macduff but that he cannot be killed by 'one of woman born', and until Birnam Wood comes to his castle.
7. Macduff flees to England to ask Malcolm to return and fight Macbeth, as Scotland is collapsing under his rule. Macbeth has Macduff's wife and children killed.
8. Lady Macbeth loses her mind and dies.
9. The castle of Macbeth is attacked by soldiers from the army of Malcolm, who prove the prediction of the witches true by using the trees of Birnam Wood as camouflage.
10. Macbeth is killed by Macduff (who we learn was delivered by Caesarean section). Malcolm is crowned king.

Making Your Own Ten Events

Before you begin, you will need to read through your script and decide on the key events of your story – ten is a good number but it could be more.

A key event is a moment that something significant changes and which moves the story forward. You should be able to express the key event in one or two sentences.

If you are developing these ten events with your cast, read them a synopsis of the play so they understand the arc of the story and decide on the key events of the play as a whole group. Then, get them into five groups and ask each group to write two events in a clear, succinct way.

Character Cards: *Macbeth*

Macbeth A brave and powerful soldier who finds out that he may become King.	**Banquo** An army general, Macbeth's loyal friend.	**Ghost** One of the characters, after they die.
Witches Supernatural beings who can see into the future.	**Duncan** The good King of Scotland.	**Birnam Wood** A forest in Scotland.
Lady Macbeth An ambitious noblewoman who wants to be Queen.	**Malcolm** The young son of the King of Scotland.	**Scotland**

INDEX OF GAMES

SKILLS

NUMBERS REFER TO GAMES NOT PAGES

6. Zounds!
7. Clap, Stamp, Shimmy
8. Venga Venga
9. Ban Ban Caliban
10. Character Swaps
13. Round Here We…
20. Tell It, See It, Map It
22. Diddly Dee
23. One-line Express
26. Iambic Pentameter Made Easy
28. Mapping
31. Sentence Types
32. Antithesis
33. Most Rare Vision
34. Image-Makers
35. Ghosting
36. This is for You
37. Yes It Is, No It Isn't
45. Leading with Body Parts
51. Reaction Box
54. Character Profiles
55. The Game of Power
57. Stop-Go
58. Three Gestures
59. Mirroring
60. Round, Across, Under
62. Flock of Birds
63. Shakespeare's Footsteps
65. Sound Orchestra

Imagination

1. I Am…
5. Shakespeare Sign Names
9. Ban Ban Caliban
11. Who's the Boss?
12. Can I Stay at Your House?
13. Round Here We…
14. Ten Events
15. Moodboarding
16. See It, Be It
17. Character Cards
18. Story Bag
20. Tell It, See It, Map It
21. Double Double
33. Most Rare Vision
34. Image-Makers
39. Improv Layers
42. Mystery Party Guest
50. The Court Makes the King
53. Strings
54. Character Profiles
65. Sound Orchestra
66. Hot Spots

Improvisation

1. I Am…
3. The Clapping Game
9. Ban Ban Caliban
11. Who's the Boss?
13. Round Here We…
14. Ten Events
16. See It, Be It
38. Punching the Line
39. Improv Layers
42. Mystery Party Guest
43. Archetypes
44. Wants and Fears
46. Role on the Wall
50. The Court Makes the King
61. Join the Dots

Memory

5. Shakespeare Sign Names
17. Character Cards
18. Story Bag
20. Tell It, See It, Map It
57. Stop-Go
60. Round, Across, Under

Physicality

4. Who's the Leader?
14. Ten Events
16. See It, Be It
34. Image-Makers
40. Barriers and Posse
43. Archetypes
45. Leading with Body Parts
46. Role on the Wall
47. Floor Surfaces
48. Shakespeare Zoo
51. Reaction Box
55. The Game of Power
56. Attract/Repel
57. Stop-Go
58. Three Gestures
59. Mirroring
60. Round, Across, Under
61. Join the Dots
62. Flock of Birds
64. Cat and Mouse

Rhythm

4. Who's the Leader?
6. Zounds!
7. Clap, Stamp, Shimmy
8. Venga Venga
21. Double Double
25. One Word Add

Storytelling

Teamwork

Voice

ALPHABETICAL LIST

NUMBERS REFER TO GAMES NOT PAGES

NOTES

NOTES

NOTES

NOTES